When I Grow Rich

A history of

Shoreditch Baptist Church

When I Grow Rich

A history of

Shoreditch Baptist Church

Christopher Voke

The Baptist Historical Society
2017

First published 2017

Spurgeon's College
189 South Norwood Hill
London SE25 6DJ
www.spurgeons.ac.uk

and

The Baptist Historical Society
Registered Office
129 Broadway, Didcot, Oxon, OX11 8RT
http://www.baptisthistory.org.uk

21 20 19 18 17 16 15 7 6 5 4 3 2 1

The right of Christopher J. Voke to be
identified as the Author of this Work has been asserted by him in
accordance with the Copyright, Designs and Patents Act 1988

All rights reserved. No part of this publication may be reproduced, stored in a retrieval system, or transmitted in any form by any means, electronic, mechanical, photocopying, recording or otherwise, without the prior permission of the publisher or a license permitting restricted copying. In the UK such licenses are issued by the Copyright Licensing Agency, 90 Tottenham Court Road, London W1P 9HE.

British Library Cataloguing in Publication Data
A catalogue record for this book is available from the British Library

ISBN 978-0-903166-45-4
Cover designed by AlphaGraphics

Printed and bound in Great Britain
by AlphaGraphics North East
www.agnortheast.com

Dedication

For years I have been fascinated by the history of our church and of Christian social reform in Tower Hamlets, the place of my birth and the place of my re-birth in Christ. Walking in the footsteps of those who went before at the Tab is as humbling as it is exciting; these ordinary men and women who achieved extraordinary acts of faith through great generosity and love.

Great men like William Cuff, who responded to the call to come and serve and who later built the big church and a School Room for the poor. It is fitting then that, exactly 100 years since Cuff's ministry at the Tab ended, our new church stands on the same spot where his was built.

I am grateful to Dr Chris Voke for his vision and perseverance in producing this history of our church. I dedicate it to all our beautiful members and friends of the Tab, past, present and still to come.

Glory to you God; greater things are yet to be done here in our city.

Rev Georgina Stride,
Shoreditch Tabernacle Baptist Church.

CONTENTS

Page

Contents
Foreword
Preface

1.	The Founders (1829 - 1838)	7
2.	The Take-over (1839 - 1853)	13
3.	The Church Goes Back Home (1854 - 1871)	19
4.	William Cuff (1872 - 1879)	28
5.	The New Tabernacle (1880 – 1884)	41
6.	A Spiritual Community with Dinners (1881 – 1896)	46
7.	Children and the School Room (1890 – 1903)	53
8.	The Sweet Air of Hackney Road (1902 – 1917)	62
9.	Spirited Sisters (1918 – 1927)	70
10.	Repair and Recovery (1928 – 1939)	79
11.	Bombed and Blessed (1940 – 1944)	89
12.	Adjusting to a Changed Future (1944 – 1947)	99
13.	Sowing so as to Reap (1946 – 1960)	103
14.	Loved for What Happened Inside (1961 – 1967)	113
15.	Social Change and Political Action (1968 – 1989)	119
16.	Land and Love in Action (1982 - 2000)	129

17.	Courage for a New Beginning (2000 - 2009)	137
18.	Transforming the Tab (2010 – 2017)	145

Appendices

Minsters of Shoreditch Baptist Church	154
Deaconesses of Shoreditch Baptist Church	155
Acknowledgements	156
Bibliography	157
Notes	163
Index	177

Foreword

This absorbing narrative tells of an important East London institution over almost two centuries. Shoreditch Baptist Church has shaped many lives, and shaped the local community too. Ernest Clifford, Minister from 1929 to 1946, summed up its vision: *'the gospel of Jesus is central but the care of the poor is essential'*.

One Church's story illuminates East London's story. Adjoining the remarkable Mildmay Hospital, Shoreditch Baptist Church hasn't been alone. Together with its network – like Victoria Park Baptist Church and East London Tabernacle in Tower Hamlets, and West Ham Central Mission in Newham – it has wielded a powerful, positive influence.

It has done an enormous amount to care for its community. It pioneered the appointment of deaconesses from 1919. It had committed members – like George Cartwright, baptised at the church in 1874, mainstay of the church's administration for fifty years, and his son George who died in 1957 after sixty years' service. But its Ministers bore a heavy burden, frequently suffering exhaustion.

We read of *'difficult years from the early sixties'*. Britain had changed. The enthusiasm, and vast congregations, of the Victorian heyday and inter-war years seemed very distant. People were moving out of London. The Church struggled to connect.

But today, another half century has passed, and times have changed again. New people have come to East London, and many more are joining them. The gospel of Jesus is central for a new generation who want to serve their community. And, in Shoreditch, as in so many other places, they have some of the best ideas for addressing today's challenges.

With a new building, new leadership, new members – and the same vision – we can look forward to Shoreditch Baptist Church shaping lives and shaping its community for many years to come.

Rt Hon Stephen Timms MP
Member of Parliament for East Ham

Preface

The history of Shoreditch Baptist Church has presented me with a continual series of surprises. The hardly-known name and enormous achievements of William Cuff and the long-forgotten and overlooked deaconesses gave humbling moments of astonishment and admiration. The more recent history with its stirring vision and determination is about to open a door to what will be a long and effective future in a very different world.

Perhaps even more I have been moved by the evident love and sacrifice of the many unknown ordinary members and leaders of this church. It is good to name and honour some of them in the record. Without doubt the strength of any local church, as well as its continuing existence, depends on countless individuals won by the love of Christ and energised by the Spirit, living for the kingdom of God in their community. It is certainly true of this church. Not every pastor who took up the call had the needed skill or strength of body for the formidable task at Shoreditch and not every member was consistently worthy, but the people as whole were resilient in the end; they never left the field defeated.

There is much to celebrate in the 180 year history of this church and far too many names and events for each one to have a mention. Even so, this generation will find examples by the score from the story of Shoreditch Baptist Church to inspire and direct them. The same Lord who won the love and moved the will of those who went before is doing the same today.

I hope you will enjoy reliving this story as much as I have in discovering it. Like the Shoreditch of the nursery rhyme, this church was never humanly rich, but its people have been rich in spirit; generous with meagre resources and endless in service to the poor. The true value of this record of their history will be to stir up that same generosity and inspire the same service for Christ and his gospel. 'When I grow rich' is reminder to the church to enter more fully into the spiritual riches of knowing Christ and then to bring him to others who need him.

Chris Voke
Spurgeon's College, 2017

6

Chapter 1

The Founders

Walk left from Shoreditch Old Town Hall in Old Street, take the next turn and you will be in Curtain Road. This is where the small congregation first met which grew into Shoreditch Baptist Church. Passing a warehouse[1] you might hear a voice, possibly the 'good and godly' Mr. James Bradley who traded  from that building, preaching to children and a group of adults. In this premises in 1829 a Sunday School for 'poor, ragged and wicked children' was started to teach them to read and know about Jesus.[2] Such schools were common in cities in the early 19th century. The Anglican school system was strengthened at this time to prevent non-conformist activists like Mr Bradley and his friends from gaining too much influence in the field.

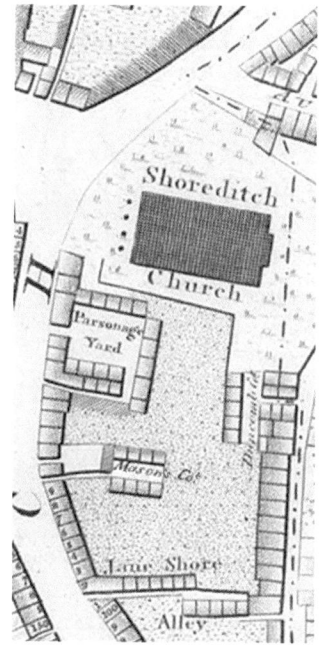

Mason's Court, off Shoreditch High Street

Very soon his work drew in adults from the district and Sunday preaching began. A warehouse was not a suitable place, so a group of men met in the home of Mr. William Perkins, a 'trimming maker' of 61 Curtain Road. They planned to find a better building for the infant church.[3] James Bradley was a shoe manufacturer and he offered a building behind his house. This was Ebenezer Chapel in Mason's Court, located at 109-11, Shoreditch High Street, twelve doors down from St Leonard's Church.[4] A London map of 1868 shows Mason's Court.[5] Bradley also built a day school which his wife ran. A member of the church, James Crisp, later records that he attended the school with his sister.

The newly formed church soon called a pastor. On Tuesday 26th June, 1832 the 'Rev Charles Bathurst Woodman[6] was ordained pastor of the Baptist Church assembling at Ebenezer Chapel, High

Street, Shoreditch, London'. A notable member in the congregation on that day was 'Mr Knibb from Jamaica'. William Knibb was a well-known Baptist missionary and passionate advocate for the ending of slavery.[7] However, this early venture with professional leadership for the church ended sadly. Woodman had been a student at the Bristol Baptist Academy, leaving after a year through ill health.[8] Then in 1831 he had been pastor of a Baptist church in Shacklewell.[9] The 25 year old pastor soon came under criticism from the Shoreditch church members. He refused to submit to any investigation of his conduct and there were no formal charges, so the matter was dropped.[10] However, the situation was not resolved and he was gone within a year. He was moneyed and influential, which may well have been why he initially impressed the local members with their limited influence and financial resources. But he was also mentally unstable and his ministry did not last very long.[11]

An entirely different period began in 1833 when James Smith, who had already been pastor at Ilford for 25 years, was called to Ebenezer Chapel. He began the development of what was to be a large and influential Baptist church. The first years led to growth and so a bigger place was urgently needed. More significant, the owner of the rented building (probably James Bradley) wanted them to 'yield their united judgments to his control'[12]. It was time to move out of Ebenezer Chapel.

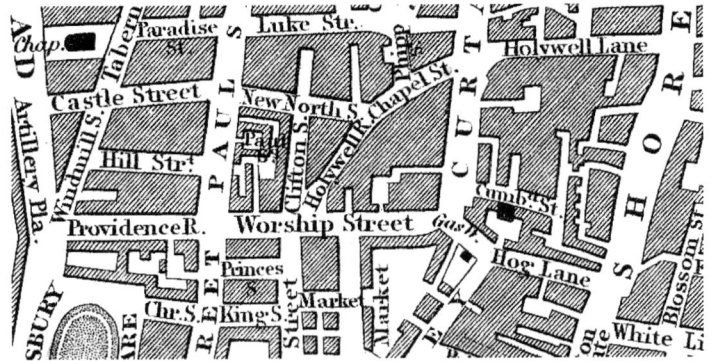

Providence Hall, or 'Union Chapel', in Cumberland (Cumb") Street

First they agreed to rent 'Providence Hall' on the south side[13] of Cumberland Street (now Hearn Street) off Curtain Road,[14] originally a Calvinistic Methodist Church. At the same time a committee was organized to find and buy land for building a chapel of their own. For £350 they obtained the freehold of the area where the present Church and the Tab Centre sits, with space beside it for a burial ground 'with a wall around'.[15] During excavations for the new development in 2015, a digger disturbed skeletons of an adult and a child with parts of a coffin. The burial ground had been in use for a short while after 1836. This was clearly the family grave of an early church member

The church drew up plans for 'a substantial and commodious chapel'.[16] It was cheekily set between St Leonard's Church and a Primitive Methodist chapel,[17] built in the space between the houses surrounding it, with a passage from Austin Street. A thousand people gathered for the laying of the corner stone on May 2nd 1836, with an address and prayer. £28 was collected.

The report of the occasion reads,

> Since they published their circular in September last the committee, whose names were then announced, have continued to meet frequently for prayer and consultation. The freehold ground has been legally conveyed to them and subscriptions donations and promises have been received by them amounting to nearly £800. The congregation has been regular and generally as large as the hall could conveniently accommodate. The members of the church have increased from 60 to 110 in ten months and the meetings of the church and congregation have been evidently characterized by Christian devotion and harmony. The dimensions of the building on the outside are 75 feet by 45 including a convenient vestry and which, together with the inclosure of the ground and sundry other unavoidable expenses for conveyance trust deeds &c, will cost about £1,800 besides the purchase of the freehold. They are aware that this is a serious undertaking and that it exceeds the calculations announced in their former appeal. The expense of the foundation has been more than they anticipated and the price of building materials has considerably advanced. But they have sought the best advice of friends and proceeded with great caution and deliberation and they are much encouraged to expect the co-operation of the Christian public around them. Donations will be thankfully received by the Pastor the Deacons and the treasurer R. Davies Esq., 190 Shoreditch, or by any member of the committee.[18]

(The deacons listed are Thomas Boulton, Nathaniel Kevan and Benjamin Skerritt.)

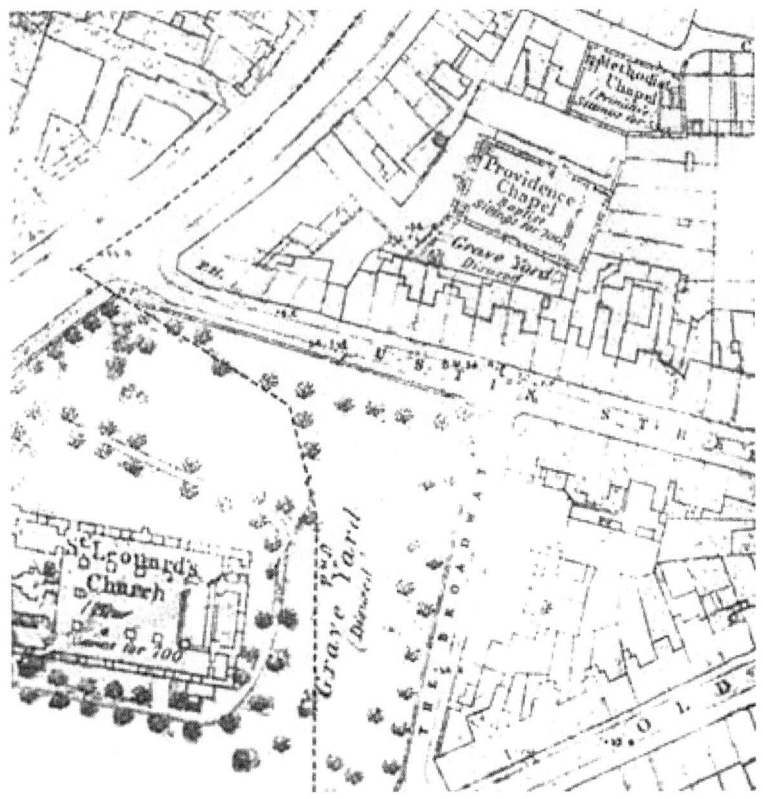

On September 20th, 1836 the new building was opened and was called (confusingly) 'Providence Chapel'. When the galleries were added it seated 6-700 people.[19] Smith recorded in April 1837,

> the attendance on the Word and ordinances at our new chapel are encouraging and the Word is evidently much blessed. Our members are increased upwards of an hundred and thirty, and we have the cheering prospect of further increase.

The congregation, as against the signed-up membership, was much greater. Smith recognized that the people contributed to the growth of the church and says, it is

> really amazing to see how ready my poor people are to do their utmost to help forward this good and great work; I believe the love of Christ constraineth them.[20]

James Smith was an excellent preacher, much in demand, and an experienced and devoted pastor. He was greatly loved by the new congregation. He lived at 7, Trafalgar Place East, a mile from Shoreditch, near present Bethnal Green Station. A letter to a friend written in May 1835 gives a flavour of his ministry and his devotion to Christ. No wonder the church grew well.

> I have as much work as I can do and might have much more if I could do it, but our powers are limited and if anything is stretched too far. Something must give way. I have four regular services at my own station weekly and had twelve preaching engagements last month. Besides these I in ten days was obliged to say 'No' to eight applications; anniversaries, ordinations, charity sermons, opening, or reopening places of worship, missionary meetings etc. I love my work. I love my Master and his service. I wish and mean to live and labour and die in it. I desire fairly to wear out, but not carelessly to tear out. I occasionally feel a little longing to be gone, but generally willing to stay as long as there is anything I can do for the honour of Jesus.[21]

However, a year later his health began to fail. He writes that pastoral visitation is hindered and he can no longer walk the mile to church and needs a carriage.[22] The congregation was still growing fast. But Smith died in August 1838 at the age of 59. He had given the church after its hesitant beginning, a very good start.

Providence Chapel built 1836. James Crisp says, 'I drew a picture of the Chapel before [in front of] the entrance, which Mr Cuff had copied and put in his book.'

Chapter 2

The Take-over

Smith's successor was the Rev. William Miall. On the 26th of November 1839 at Providence Chapel, Shoreditch, he was 'set apart to the pastoral office over the church late under the care of our deceased friend the Rev James Smith'. The new chapel was crowded for the occasion and the 'very interesting' services were conducted by local ministers and notable Baptists.[1] In spite of this early enthusiasm 54 discontented members left within two years. After a brief time meeting in a former independent Methodist 'Middlesex' Chapel, King Street (now Diss Street) off Hackney Road,[2] this group formed a congregation which went back to their old place, Providence Hall, Cumberland Street.[3]

This separated group adopted the title 'Union Church', an original name of the Cumberland Street building. On April 25th 1846 they took a lease on the chapel, two tenements, and the 'school room'. Oddly 'the organ is excepted'. The signatories were Nathaniel Kevan, Benjamin Robert (gent), Robert Sowdell (bookseller), John Millard (upholsterer) and Thomas Pillow.[4] Pillow was a 'lighterman', the owner of a fleet of barges on the Thames. Pillow and Kevan, who we meet again, emerge as significant leaders in the future church. They later signed the letter inviting William Cuff to be pastor. James Crisp, a long-time member of the church, remembered he was 'taken when a little boy' and knew the notable leaders' names.[5]

These men and the congregation with them are the true ancestors of the present Church since, as we shall see, they returned later to James Smith's Providence Chapel and so became Shoreditch Baptist Church. They left of their own free will, and were formally 'dismissed', that is, removed from the membership, on 26th October 1841.[6] The reasons for their decision to leave are hard to discern. The popular James Smith was a difficult man to follow. Miall was not as gifted a preacher, nor so eager an evangelist. He was certainly more scholarly, as his later discourses 'on religious truth' show. In 1841 on his second anniversary he was presented by the members with 'a copy of *Home's Introduction to the Critical Study and Knowledge of the Holy Scriptures* (in 4 volumes) as a testimony of their attachment and esteem.'[7] He started a 'Congregational Library' with a committee formed of the deacons and six others. There were very few subscribers, possibly only the members of the committee.[8] Later Miall published scholarly books; a book on eternal punishment in 1869 and *Phases of Religion, Addresses on the*

Form of Religion Proper to Various Periods of Life in 1884. All this did not go down very well with the cobblers and furniture craftsmen of Shoreditch, who remembered the vibrant and earthy James Smith.

The Development of Shoreditch Baptist Church, 1829-69

Curtain Road Ragged School (1829 -)

Ebenezer. Mason's Court.

Charles Bathurst Woodman
James Smith (pastor 1833-38)

Evicted from Ebenezer. Moved to 'Providence Hall', Worship Street (Cumberland St) (1835)

Built Providence Chapel. Austin Street

William Miall (pastor 1839-52)

54 members leave to King St, then 'Union Chapel', Cumberland Street (1840)

Hugh Killen (pastor 43-47)

Charles Smith (pastor 48-53)

Providence Chapel taken over by Smith's 'Union' Church

Charles Smith (pastor 1853-56)

Miall and 176 members leave to form Queen's Road, Dalston (1852)

Smith and 65 members leave to form a church in 'Providence Hall', Cumberland Street

William Miall (pastor 1852-92)   **John Russell (pastor 1856-69)**   **Charles Smith (pastor 56 -59)**

Church disappears by 1859

The reasons for division were thus personal, but they were also doctrinal. Miall was not as thorough a Calvinist, nor even as careful a Baptist, as his people expected. Later he questioned the doctrine of eternal punishment.[9] He was not as strict over membership and communion as the members wished; unbaptised people were allowed to take communion.[10] More troubling, he was favourable to the idea that denominational doctrine should be set aside for unity. In 1869 he joined the 'The Free Christian Union' and shared a platform with its founder, James Martineau, who tried to unite all Christians under a universally accepted doctrine of God. This organization did not last. Many involved became Unitarians (who deny orthodox theology of the Trinity).[11]

Even more serious were Miall's spiritualist connections. He became a council member of the British National Association of Spiritualists. He was even invited in 1880 to be the president of the Dalston branch. There is no record of him accepting.[12] He was clearly a free thinker. Some might argue he was merely unwise, ahead of his time and willing to experiment, though basically orthodox in faith and churchmanship. However, if he was inclined to such ideas, or hinted at them from the pulpit, it is not surprising that his members objected strongly, that many left and that the church eventually declined under his teaching.

Nevertheless in his first seven years at Shoreditch those who stayed with Miall grew to over two hundred members. There was very strict discipline. Members were regularly excluded from communion, or 'erased' after being visited by two 'Brethren'. Reasons given are: for being 'habitually guilty of the sin of intoxication' or of 'falsehood', for 'disorderly conduct', or if they did not 'fill up their place' at the Lord's Supper for three months. Deacons were needed and two more were appointed.[13] There were regular weeknight baptism services. A 'Benevolent Society' was active in the district and a 'Maternal Society' run by Miall's wife Eliza and Mrs James Miall, their daughter in law.

In spite of debt remaining on the chapel, in 1843 the deacons told the church the Pastor's income was 'inadequate to meet his necessities'. The church meeting would only agree to give him a gift of £15, 'part of the balance in hand on the Burial Ground Account'. They also arranged to meet for prayer about the finances.[14] These were signs of financial and relationship difficulties to come. The debt on Providence Chapel was finally cleared in May 1844.[15] But the Sunday School now had an average attendance of two hundred. So by a majority vote 'of the male members of the church' it was resolved to build a much needed Sunday School and Lecture Room for 'the instruction of the children in religious truth in order to the conversion of their souls to God'.[16] It was nearly finished by October. There was also a mission school in Thorold

Square, Bethnal Green with 120 children on the books. By 1849 the debt on the School Room was largely discharged.[17]

Miall was clearly a good leader and committed to prayer, which he repeatedly encouraged in the church. The church continued to attract many. There were regular baptisms. New members joined in a steady flow; but they flowed out with similar regularity. Miall's preaching was not attractive to the working people of Shoreditch. He introduced a plan to use handbills for publicity 'with a view to increasing the attendance' on Sundays.[18] Numbers still decreased in services and membership losses followed, many for 'non-attendance'.[19] Much needed income decreased and additional costs were incurred on building alterations and repairs.[20] In spite of radical fundraising plans the debts remained. Attendance was weak at Church Meetings. There was debate about the 'mode of conducting the singing' on Sundays.[21]

The people drifted off, some to join former friends at Cumberland Street. By the middle of 1851 Miall told the deacons that he intended to resign because of 'the extreme irregularity of attendance of members at the ordinary services.' The deacons, generally on Miall's side, persuaded him to reconsider. However, he wanted the members 'to express their feelings and convictions in relation to the ministry'. He told the members' meeting that if there was 'a considerable minority who were dissatisfied, or desirous of change, he should feel it his duty to resign and if there was no improvement in attendance he would certainly resign'. A show of hands gave Miall unanimous support. The church also promised that they would do better and would 'exert all their influence to secure the regular attendance of others'.[22]

The plan did not work. In early 1852 money to pay the pastor was running out.[23] Miall and the deacons had 'repeated consultations on the habitual smallness of the congregations'. In May at a special Church Meeting they told the members they thought this was 'attributable to the situation of our place of worship'. They had developed a strategy to move out of Providence Chapel. A new and more suitable location in the Dalston area was proposed, so that a larger congregation might be attracted. They also told the members that at Providence Hall, Cumberland Street the lease was running out and their former members now worshipping there might be interested in occupying Providence Chapel. A figure of £1200 would be asked of the Cumberland Street people, which would go towards building a new chapel for Miall. The discussion on this challenging proposal was protracted. No decision was taken.[24] By the next meeting in June it came to a head. The vote resulted in a large majority for moving out. A building committee was appointed to look for a suitable site in the Queen's Place area of Dalston,[25] at the time 'a recently increased suburban village, with some handsome houses'.[26]

The next part of the story requires some careful following. You may like to refer to the chart on page 14. The legal problem of the trustees of one church selling their building to another group was got over by a simple device. Some members of Cumberland Street would be admitted to membership of Providence Chapel. Then the members of the Providence Chapel church, who wished to move location, could transfer out to form a new church with William Miall. At the Church Meeting in August 1852 this was begun. It was announced that the Cumberland Street church agreed to give £1200 'for the liquidation of the debt on the schoolroom' and towards the building fund for Miall's new church. Then 211 members were admitted from Cumberland Street to Providence church. A tea meeting was arranged for the members to be 'mutually introduced'.[27] The process was not without elements of friendliness and grace.

The combined membership met on September 14th. It was a dramatic occasion. About 130 members of the Cumberland Street church turned up, along with Charles Smith their pastor. Miall and his church counted 50 who had come. He vacated the chair which was then taken by Smith. A letter, apparently signed by 176 Providence Chapel members was read, asking for 'dismission' to form a church in Queen's Road (now Queensbridge Road). This was agreed and Miall informed them that £1200 had been paid to the treasurer of their building fund. It was agreed that Miall and his 'new' church could hire the Chapel, School Room and Chapel House at £2-10-0 a month, for continued use until their new chapel was built. Miall then left the meeting with his 50 members. Charles Smith stood aside and Nathaniel Kevan presided as the church elected Smith as future Pastor of Providence Chapel.[28] The exchange was done.

A significant matter emerged at the same meeting which was to have long and damaging consequences. The £1200 had been borrowed on 5% interest from individuals not named. It was agreed that newly elected deacons (Kevan, Sandell, Thomas Pillow, William Pope and Joseph Harnden) would give their names as security for the debt. The church agreed 'to pledge itself to support our Brethren in the liability thus incurred'.

It is difficult to interpret what this move to the Victorian suburbs was truly about. In Miall's early years the church had prospered. But the evidence all points to the fact that he and his leaders, though adept managers and worthy men, were not at home with Shoreditch and its people. Nor did they grasp how great an opportunity there was to serve the densely housed multitude of working people, often desperately poor, who surrounded Austin Street. The next generation of leaders did.

Conversely, on the whole the congregation did not find the scholarly and aspiring middle class approach of Miall and his leaders to their taste. They were also not inspired, or entertained, by his preaching, or they suspected his doctrine. So they stopped coming and ceased giving. There is one telling comment in the minutes of the members meeting where the proposal to move was put. It was stated that when they built the new church in a better area 'the major part of our present members [would] be able to attend'. This was either blindness, or deliberate deception. The Queen's Road Chapel to be built was more than a mile north of Shoreditch in a very different area. In a time when everyone except the very wealthy had to walk, the idea that the majority would now forsake their old chapel and travel a further mile or more out of their natural context was unrealistic.

Queen's Road Baptist Church, Dalston

The group who left became Queen's Road Baptist Church, Dalston. Miall remained its pastor for nearly 40 years. The survey of 1887 has his morning congregation as 62 and the evening as 78. The same survey has Cuff at Shoreditch with 1453 morning and 1448 evening congregations. The conclusion is that William Miall's first instinct to resign was right; his ministry was not working at Shoreditch. Sadly it did not truly work at Dalston either.

Smith's people went back to worship at Cumberland Street for the time being, but using Providence Chapel for Members' Meetings. Immediately a trickle of members began to leave Miall and move to Smith's church, which some months later took possession of Providence Chapel. An Opening Service was held on Sunday 27th March 1853 and a Tea Meeting 'to give friends the opportunity of selecting their sittings in the Chapel'. Shoreditch Baptist Church seemed able at last to settle down; but not entirely.

Chapter 3

The Church Goes Back Home

So who was Charles Smith and what is the story of the group who left Providence Chapel, Austin Street in 1841 and came home again after twelve years? We need to backtrack and tell this part of the story since they are the true ancestors of Shoreditch Baptist Church. (See chart of the development of the church above.)

The group of 54 members who left Miall and Providence Chapel in 1841 set up their church back in the old hall in Cumberland Street off Curtain Road, between number 18 and 19.[1] This was a useful building with 'New Rooms' used for smaller meetings and a 'Chapel House' adjoining.[2] The church was soon under the pastoral care of a man named Hugh Killen. The church flourished and grew to over 200 members by 1853. Indications are that this church was tighter about church membership and more careful over doctrine than at Providence Chapel, Austin Street. Killen and his church were Calvinistic in their doctrine. They were already 'particular' rather than 'general' Baptists. That is, their doctrine of election and redemption included the idea that God chose 'particular' people for whom Christ died (so not everyone in 'general') and who were therefore destined to be saved. But they were also 'strict'; they admitted as members only people baptized as believers and they allowed only members to take communion. Hence they were by name and practice 'Strict and Particular Baptists'. The original church at Providence Chapel was on the side of the 'Particular Baptists', but as we have seen, this Cumberland Street group were not convinced that William Miall and his people were firm enough about these matters. So they departed.

Killen was very committed to the firmer stance. The Cumberland Street chapel in 1846 was the venue for the launch of The London Association of Strict Baptist Ministers and Churches. Killen was a founding member. Six churches joined, most Baptist churches did not. The Cumberland Street church was accepted.[3] Nathaniel Kevan, now one of the respected leaders at Cumberland Street became their 'messenger', or representative, to the Association. For a short while he was treasurer. The Association was founded to combat doctrinal and church laxity; 'in consequence of the spread of general redemption and free-communion in our churches.'[4] In 1848 Killen was called away to be minister of Mill Lane, Bedford, a church formerly led by John Bunyan and previously an open communion church. The members of Mill Lane now 'thought that it was more consistent and scriptural that the communion of the church should be confined to persons baptized on a profession of their faith in Christ and that open communion had led to laxity of doctrine.' Killen certainly suited their changed approach.[5] At Cumberland Street these policies had formed, in a very deprived area of London, a robust and distinctive membership. Five years later, and much stronger, they returned and took over Shoreditch Baptist Church in Providence Chapel, Austin Street.

In June 1848 Charles Smith, who had been pastor at a Particular Baptist Church in Mill Road near Tring, came to Cumberland Street. Churches at the time were wary of calling someone without testing out their preaching and doctrine for a while. Smith was invited 'to supply the pulpit for six months'. He began to do so on Sunday 18th of June. He found favour with the church before the time was up and accepted the invitation of the church to take the pastorate. He 'entered upon his pastoral duties on Lord's day the 19th of Nov'.[6] The church was progressing well with a full programme of services: Sundays 10.45 a.m. and 6.30 p.m., Monday prayer at 7.00 p.m. and a Wednesday service with preaching at 7.00 p.m. The Lord's Supper was observed on the first Sunday evening of the month. Seats for services could be booked and paid for in advance, as was the custom, at the Chapel House.[7]

Even now there were signs of future problems, because of Smith's theology and those who supported him. Being very strict about doctrine and church membership has a down side. How strict do you need to be? If someone disagrees with you over 'particular redemption' can you still worship and work with them? The more strict and particular you are the smaller and smaller your Christian world becomes. Some decided they could not continue with the 'London Association of Strict Baptist Ministers and Churches', small and strict as it was. Kevan stopped attending and Smith was not supportive of it. The church eventually withdrew in spite of a delegation to the deacons of the church.[8] Then in 1849 four churches, including Smith and Cumberland Street, formed 'The London New Association of Strict and Particular Baptists'.[9]

The Cumberland Street church continued to flourish and grow. This is not surprising. The population of Shoreditch was increasing faster than any other London parish: from 35,000 in 1801 to 130,000 in 1852 and almost doubling between 1831 and 1861. This church of 211 members, under strict discipline, plus the wider congregation, was robustly and prayerfully led by doctrinally committed leaders. They were well placed to make an offer to take over Shoreditch Baptist Church in Providence Chapel, Austin Street.

So now we can revisit the end of the dramatic meeting of September 14th, 1852. William Miall left the meeting and the church immediately elected Charles Smith as pastor. His deacons also were elected to office for the new Chapel.[10] The church was already a 'Particular Baptist Church' and the articles of faith were strongly Calvinistic. But there were ominous signs of continuing tension over doctrine, church practice and wider association. The church adopted a twelve-point Calvinistic doctrinal basis. At the members' meeting in October the church voted to affirm the 'closed communion' principle, which they observed had been neglected previously at Providence Chapel. The stricter elements of the Cumberland Street church, including Smith, began to shift the theology of the church. From then onwards only church members, properly baptised as believers of course, would be allowed to take communion.

In 1853 a prolonged debate began over the proposal that the church should join the London New Association of Strict and Particular Baptists, which Smith favoured. Myall's church had not been a member of this Association, so Smith wanted formally now to join it. The members were not entirely with him in his views. The proposal finally failed with a split vote in January. The numbers recorded are 7 for and 9 against. The explanation for such a small vote is that only the votes of the 21 'brethren' listed as present were counted, with five abstentions. The women were not allowed to vote. Was Smith unhappy about this result? It seems so.

However, the church was generally functioning well. The leadership was strong and the members committed. A good number were involved in the business of the church. There were still members regularly visited for non-attendance, but the membership numbers were sustained. A 'young Brother' Samuel Kevan, probably Nathaniel's nephew, was thought to 'possess preaching gifts which ought to be encouraged by the church'. He was invited to preach after a prayer meeting. He did so with great acceptance, was asked again and was formally approved by the church.[11]

C. H. Spurgeon aged 23

In this period the 23 year old Charles Spurgeon agreed to preach an Anniversary Sermon in Providence Chapel. On a Tuesday evening in 1855 the chapel, built to hold six hundred, was packed with eight or nine hundred people. A huge crowd also was out in the small courtyard. Spurgeon records that when he '*personally* appealed to the throng outside, disappointed at not getting in, most of them dispersed, and allowed the rest of us to worship as well as we could with the windows open to let those hear who remained outside.'[12] He returned to the area in June and on Tuesday 22nd preached in a field in Hackney (King Edward's Road) to about 10,000 people. He only escaped the cheering crowd when he saw two strangers in an open carriage nearby. He 'sprang in, and begged them to drive away'.[13]

The church that had run well at Cumberland Street now began to stagger. Smith was not as inspiring a preacher as was needed for the new context and the next stage of growth. The later pastor, William Cuff, had heard Smith preach and commented unkindly that 'if he was as dry and dreary as he was when I heard him sometimes at Cheltenham, I am not surprised he did not succeed at Providence'.[14] Ominously, at some point Smith had added his name, in the sum of £100, to stand security for the Bond of £1200 borrowed for the purchase of the chapel. He was clearly not in the financial position to do so and this became increasingly 'a burden on his mind'.[15]

There were continuing financial pressures on the church. The generally poor membership did not respond to pay off the large debt from their purchase of the Chapel, nor could they sustain the extra expense of a larger church. There was a 'pew opener', paid £3.00 a year. Someone was paid £8.00 to conduct the singing at services. It was proposed in July 1855 that both these were now to work unpaid. The Chapel Keeper, with rent free use of the Chapel House and £15 a year, had his wage cut to £12. Appeals were put in magazines for funds. Charles Smith was absent from this meeting. The members agreed to 'respectfully request him to relinquish £20 per annum' from his £120 salary 'while the difficulty lasted'. The steady Nathaniel Kevan and Thomas Pillow were deputed to go and ask him. Smith fatally replied in writing to this proposal. He 'would rather quietly resign his Pastorate than submit to what he deemed was an unreasonable request'. The church decided to 'unhesitatingly abandon' the idea.[16]

Seeds of conflict had been sown, however, and they came to fruition on 27th December 1855. Charles Smith stood up in the Church Meeting and read a list of grievances against the deacons. The deacons then protested that they had not intended to interfere 'with the Pastor's duties or comfort' and one by one immediately resigned. The Pastor then asked for a vote of confidence. The vote failed. So he resigned, mentioning specifically his £100 security, which he wished the church to cover. He then left the meeting, but not before the church asked him to take the services one last time the following Sunday. On 30th December, at the end of the evening service, Smith read out a statement giving his interpretation of events. The deacons, in a reply which was read out in church the following Sunday, labelled his action 'highly censurable' and the content 'a gross misrepresentation of the facts'.[17]

There was no recovering such a breakdown. Within a month Smith and 65 members sent a letter asking 'honourable dismission' from Providence Chapel to form 'a church of Christ of the same faith and order with yourselves'.[18] The church agreed, but expressed regret that these 'whom they love in the Lord should allow themselves to be so misguided by misrepresentation from the pulpit without affording their brethren an opportunity of vindicating themselves from charges brought against them in so unchristianlike a manner.'[19] Smith and his group went back to worship at Cumberland Street.[20] The new church did not last long and had disappeared from all records by 1859.

It is difficult for us today to discern the reasons for such a split. There were certainly personality and communication issues, as reflected in Cuff's comments about Smith's preaching. The longer divisions were doctrinal. The newly formed Providence Chapel congregation was not so concerned about strict communion. They had been persuaded, perhaps against their better judgment, by the pastor to apply a policy of 'closed communion'. As we shall see, they quite comfortably reversed this decision later.

You wonder how a church with such a conflicted record can survive. Is it the sheer grace of God? Is it the sustaining power of the gospel? It was clearly being preached, the members were being fed and they were faithful in life and witness. A further answer is the group of truly godly, sincere and trustworthy men and women who worked to see matters through. One of these was Nathaniel Kevan.

Nathaniel Kevan

It is worth dwelling on his story, since he links together this turbulent period in the church. His life is also a reflection of early 19th century London. He illustrates the doctrinally conflicted church experience of many people of that time, but he comes out the end still serving and honoured as a Christian man and Baptist leader. Nathaniel was a slater. This was a good trade in Shoreditch, with massive house building projects going on. Born in 1799 in Southwark, he married 21 year old

Phebe Pask from Curtain Road in 1822 and moved to Shoreditch. They soon had two children. Then Phebe died. There were several major epidemics at that time: smallpox in 1825, 'one of the more severe visitations',[21] typhoid in 1826. Densely populated Shoreditch had high figures of deaths from these outbreaks and the death of his young wife from one of these is highly likely.

Two years later Nathaniel married her 20 year old sister Elizabeth. Here his life touches on one of the repeated controversies of Victorian England. By Anglican Church law a man was prohibited from marrying the sister of his deceased wife. The Marriage Act of 1835 had made this principle firm, although it recognized marriages existing before this date. So Kevan was legally off the hook. The 'deceased wife law' was petitioned against in May 1850 by congregations of Protestant dissenters, including Cumberland Street, where Kevan was a leader.[22] They did not want the law used to prosecute, or disadvantage good people married in this way. Kevan was one of these and would definitely have voted to join the petition. With others in his church he raised it again in 1858 when the Providence Chapel church meeting agreed to petition the Government.[23] The prohibition was not finally removed until 1907. Nathaniel had seven further children with Elizabeth; in spite of legal questions, a sign of God's blessing.

Nathaniel was involved in the very start of Shoreditch Baptist Church. In 1835 he was 36 and already a deacon of James Smith in Ebenezer Chapel, Mason's Court. He was part of the expanding church that moved to Cumberland Street and was present as a deacon during the great days of development, purchasing the land and building Providence Chapel.[24] His oldest daughter (also Phebe) married Smith's son Josiah (1845). Kevan bore the early death of his much-loved pastor and continued to serve the church. He stopped attending Sunday worship soon after Miall's arrival. As a wise leading member he seemed to see what would happen under Miall's ministry. He was 'put under visitation for non-attendance' in January 1842 and then 'erased' from the Church Book because he had 'united with an Independent Chapel'.[25]

He had joined with the people who left Miall and Providence in 1839 to set up again in Cumberland Street. He is named with others in the purchase of the chapel and other buildings.[26] He continued as a deacon with Hugh Killen and became his church's representative, or 'messenger' to the Association of Strict Baptist Churches. He led prayer at these meetings and was elected treasurer. He survived the Strict Baptist doctrinal tangles of that period with his faith still intact. He was back in Providence Chapel with Charles Smith as one of the deacons when they all returned and took over the church. During this period he gradually improved his situation. He was no longer a jobbing slater, but a 'collector' working for The Imperial Gas Company. In his work he had access to cash and was instrumental in discerning some customers' frauds.[27]

A trustworthy and reliable man, he became highly respected in the community. In his final years, still a faithful member of Providence Chapel, he was elected and re-elected a 'vestryman' of St Leonard's Parish[28] and sat on the Paving, Lighting and Sanitary Committee. The Vestry was an early form of local council, not a religious body, responsible for checking and overseeing public works. Shoreditch was foremost in London in this desperately needed task: providing clean water, improving sanitation and removing 'nuisances', such as pigs kept in the back yards of the densely built terraces. It is not hard to imagine gracious and reliable Nathaniel persuading poor and suspicious local tenants to do what was needed to improve their lives.

He was a quiet man, not recorded as contributing much to the Vestry discussions. At the same time he was presenting an attractive face of Baptist life and witness. He fades from view in the church minutes, after 1858, his active witness lay elsewhere in his community duties. He died on January 4th, 1862 and is buried in Abney Park Cemetery, Stoke Newington. His epitaph from Proverbs 10 reads, 'The memory of the just is blessed'. His obituary states;

> It is with great regret that we have to announce the death of Mr. Nathaniel Kevan, a gentleman well known in Shoreditch, and universally respected. The melancholy event took place on Saturday last, after an illness of a few months. He had been for many years a collector for the Independent Gas Company and by his urbanity of manner and attention to his duties obtained the highest respect, both from the company and its customers. He was a member of the Shoreditch Vestry from its commencement, and on the two – or three, we forget which - occasions he was elected, we believe he obtained the highest number of votes recorded in the Church Ward, which he represented. He was held in the highest esteem by the Vestry, and his loss will be regretted by all who knew him.'[29]

Christian social and political action, combined with strong gospel witness is amply illustrated by the life of this faithful Baptist layman. The culture of a Baptist church deeply engaged with its community was to continue.

Providence Chapel needed a new minister. The deacons advertised in *The Freeman*, the brand new Baptist weekly newspaper. They received 20 replies. In spite of its recent enormous upheaval, the church was an attractive proposition to a prospective pastor. He would have a large congregation of families in a populous district. In June, 1856 John Russell of Clover Street, Chatham accepted a unanimous invitation to the pastorate.[30] The church judged him to be 'the most likely minister we have yet heard to become a successful labourer in this locality'.[31]

Their judgement proved right. Russell was, 'a theologian of the old type' who thought nothing of preaching two sermons every Sunday over an hour long. Not a very moderate Calvinist, he 'hammered away at the old doctrines', grew strong men, and left them in Shoreditch.[32] One of them was James Crisp, who he baptized in 1860.[33] Russell gave thirteen years of 'honest and thoughtful labour' and laid a good foundation for what was to follow.[34] Ten years later Cuff wrote that, 'from this date the day dawned' and that Russell was still 'held in reverent and grateful respect by all who enjoyed his ministry'.[35] He later preached at the closing meetings in Providence Chapel and was present at the last communion service.[36] Then he attended the opening of Cuff's Tabernacle in 1879.[37] Russell left the church stronger and more secure,[38] yet in spite of significant and continuing growth the church was financially weak. After discussion, in August 1858, 'pew rents' were ended and monthly offerings gave way to a stress on weekly offerings.[39]

John Russell, pastor 1856-69

The next pastor was Rev William C. Jones, who resigned after two years and went to Melbourne, Australia. Cuff remarks later that he was 'feeble in health' and states kindly, 'Mr Jones' ministry was not suited to the place, or the place to it. He did not succeed, and wisely resigned after a short pastorate.'[40]

There is a 'singular and rather startling story' which may explain his early departure. His wife 'turned Romanist', took away his two sons (13 and 15) and placed them in the care of Jesuits in Cornwall. Jones arrived in England in June 1880 and tried to get them back. His successor at Shoreditch, William Cuff, stood as referee for his good character. The family was briefly reunited, but, in spite of a court order by Lord Chief Justice Pollock, Mrs Jones fled again and Jones returned alone 'with a sore heart, but with a quiet conscience' to Australia.'[41]

A later comment on the early period of the church suggests that the pastors, on the whole, did not fit well with the social context of the Chapel. They 'had been very particular in regard to their doctrine; but aught [anything] like aggressive work among the mass of the poor and of the working classes, whose homes were in crowded streets all around, never seemed to occur to them.'[42] That may be a harsh assessment, but the history of the pastors so far, with two notable exceptions, seems to justify it.

While Jones was doing his best against the odds briefly to pastor the church, another story was developing. It leads directly to the great days of Shoreditch Baptist Church. William Cuff was already being courted by the church to be the next minister.

Chapter 4

William Cuff

William Cuff was born in the village of Hasfield near Tewkesbury in Gloucestershire on the 22nd February 1841. He became a 'tripe dresser' for a butcher in Cheltenham and belonged to the Baptist Church in Cambray Place. He heard Charles Spurgeon preach from a wagon in a meadow at Naunton, on the Cotswold Hills when he was 'but a lad, just then converted to God' (1862). He records, 'I there and then vowed that I would preach Jesus Christ as he did, if that could be possible to me.'[1] When Spurgeon later visited his church, Cuff stood in the packed aisle to listen, and his developing call and gifts as a local preacher became a decision about a lifetime of ministry. The next time Spurgeon visited he 'interviewed' Cuff and so in 1864 he began study at the 'Pastors' College'.[2] Spurgeon's influence on young men like William Cuff and their churches is incalculable. He later wrote of Spurgeon and of the opportunity to train;

> I loved our glorified President from the first time I met him, and I have always said that, under God, I owe to him everything I have done in the Lord's work. The Shoreditch Tabernacle is his far more than it is mine, for it would never have been built but for C. H. Spurgeon. What could I have been, or done, but for the Pastors' College? Those who knew me in my early days know best what the College did for me. I can only lovingly and gratefully revere the memory of Mr. Spurgeon, and bless the Lord that I ever knew him.[3]

After college, Cuff went first to Ridgemount, Bedfordshire, and then to Bury St Edmunds. In both churches his preaching and leadership led to immediate blessing and growth.

Spurgeon was watching. And he knew Shoreditch. He had preached at Providence Chapel in 1855 on that memorable Tuesday evening service.[4] When John Russell left Shoreditch in 1869, Spurgeon matched up the church with his 28 year old protégé. On April 20th, Thomas Pillow wrote to Cuff on behalf of the deacons.

> My Dear Sir,
> Our pastor, Rev John Russell, of Providence Chapel, Hackney Road, is about to take leave of us early next month. We have conferred with the Rev C. H. Spurgeon respecting our future,

and he has recommended us to ask you to supply for us for a
Lord's Day. If agreeable to you could you make it convenient
to come up, and supply our pulpit on the third Lord's Day in
May; should that day be inconvenient to you, perhaps you
would be good enough to say what day you could come up.
I am, my dear Sir,
Yours sincerely,
   Thomas Pillow.

Thomas Pillow, Thames barge-owner, twice Master of the Company of Watermen and Lightermen

Oliver Bridge. The deacon in whose house Cuff first met the church leaders.

Cuff was fully engaged at Bury St Edmunds and declined to 'come up'. Three years later they tried again. This time Cuff agreed to come and preach at Providence Chapel on 23rd Feb 1872.[5] However, old controversy was to prevent progress. He met the deacons for tea the previous day at the home of Oliver Bridge in Farleigh Road, Stoke Newington and discovered that that Providence was a closed communion church. He told them he could not become the Pastor since he was of the opposite view. He cheekily begged to be relieved of preaching the next day, as it would be a delight to go and listen to Mr. Spurgeon. The deacons would not hear of it and so in the morning William Cuff entered the pulpit of Providence Chapel for the first time. He began with a clear statement of his position to the congregation of about seventy-five people:

> Dear brethren, I wish to be in an honest position today. Your good deacons told me last night that you are a Strict Baptist

Church. Such are my views that nothing would induce me to become Pastor of any church under such conditions. I will preach the Gospel to you today and then wish you every blessing.[6]

The strict communion matter was a hot debate among 19th century Baptists. Cuff writes of the controversy in Bury St Edmunds, where his senior pastor Cornelius Elven had 'modified his views on Calvinism' and moved to an open communion view. He tried to get his church to change. They refused. So he wrote a little book called *Seven Reasons for Free Communion at the Table of the Lord with all them that love our Lord Jesus Christ in sincerity*. Opponents 'bought as many copies of the book as they could get and, on a village green not far from Bury St Edmunds, burned them'. Elven and Cuff later managed to 'open the Communion table, and the old controversy died.'[7]

Of his first visit to Shoreditch Cuff wrote, 'That first service seemed to me cold and poor. The Chapel looked small and dirty.' He also noted that 'the congregation looked wise, and quite theological,'[8] which implies a problem rather than a benefit. This observation confirms the view that the congregation which existed was not the class of people who Cuff later gathered in such vast numbers, but rather a people shaped by the strongly Calvinistic John Russell.

In spite of this bad start, he received a unanimous invitation for a trial of three months. Cuff declined. Later that year the church changed their rules and Providence Chapel became an open communion church. Immediately the church 'cordially and affectionately' invited him again. This time, after encouragement from Spurgeon, Cuff accepted.[9] He intended 'to preach Jesus Christ and him crucified that the church may be fed and that souls may be won'.[10] He later wrote, 'my heart was at Providence Chapel and sure I am to this day that the Lord led me back to the place where he meant to bless me.'[11]

The young William Cuff

In his brief autobiography Cuff relates an incident from his early years of preaching in Gloucestershire. It illustrates that he was not, or by his language did not seem to be, sufficiently Calvinist for some people.

> One Sunday night we had a service in a village chapel where the people stood straight for orthodoxy. They thought they understood Calvinism, and liked it. I conducted the service and thought I had got on better than usual. At the close I announced a prayer meeting, and left it open for anyone to pray. One or two prayed at once, and one good old man felt moved to speak thus unto the Lord:
> 'O Lord have mercy on the young man that have prached to us, and tach un the truth, and close every pulpit against him till a knows the truth.'[12]

The Cuffs moved to Shoreditch with their five children. Cuff's first wife Rachel (Tuff) had died early, leaving him with a son Walter Sydney, now twelve years old, born in Hasfield. The family lived at 5, Palestine Place, Cambridge Heath.[13] The ministry began on Sunday October 6th. At the very first prayer meeting there were five members present,[14] but week on week the congregation grew. On the fourth Sunday he arrived up the alley, which at some stage had been opened up into the Hackney Road, to find the Chapel packed.

He records:

> The space in front of the Chapel, a sort of yard was full. I reached the scene at twenty minutes to 11 and tried to get in. This greeted me,
> 'Who are you pushing, governor? You can't get in'.
> 'Very well', said I, 'will you please let me get to the chapel-keeper's house? I want to speak to him'.

He got into the vestry and continues:

> I can see the dear old deacons now. They were reverent, gracious men, and kind as a mother to me. That morning they did not know what to do or say. I suggested one should pray, and he did with the deepest emotion. It was a sweet benediction to me.[15]

On the fifth Sunday the Chapel was 'perfectly crowded'. Sunday morning and evening services continued, but on 23rd October Cuff had announced to the members that additional afternoon services would be held in the assembly room at the newly built Vestry Hall, now known as the Town Hall.[16] It seated 800.[17] By the end of October they saw the Hall 'crowded to suffocation'.[18] These services continued in November and then were resumed for January, along with a week of prayer and a further week of special New Year meetings at the Chapel. One estimate says that there were 1700-1800 people at the Sunday afternoon service on 26th January, 1873. (This may be exaggeration if the Vestry Hall officially seated 800 comfortably, but they were no doubt squashed in the gallery and probably standing around the walls.)

Shoreditch 'Vestry Hall' (The Town Hall) in 1873.

Some claimed Cuff went to the Town Hall to gain a large congregation. There was in fact a regular Christian meeting there already. But Cuff rightly argued that the Chapel could not hold the numbers that came. He said, 'The crowds were simply eager to hear the Word, and many of all sorts have been converted'.[19] As with all successful churches, it was claimed he won members from other churches. This was true, but the records show that most new members were baptised and joined the church from non-church backgrounds. In spite of a review of 'non-attenders' resulting in 37 erasures in November, the membership grew. By the end of 1873, 177 new members had been added to Providence Chapel. In 1875 the recorded membership was 461.

Pastoral care and nurture of the larger numbers became urgent. Cuff organized monthly special meetings for new converts.[20] The leading deacon, Oliver Bridge, laid out a further plan in December. They would print a list of all members and divide the church into six districts 'for the purpose of facilitating visiting in cases of sickness or other causes'. Six men were named to act as visitors, although he was not prepared at the time to name the six 'sisters' also to be appointed. But the whole church meeting agreed without further delay.[21]

At this same church meeting a man who was to become a significant, though lowly servant of the church was proposed for baptism. His name was Job Wren and he lived at 47, Peabody Building, Spitalfields. These were low-rent apartments built in 1864 to 'ameliorate the condition of the poor and needy' in London. We have no account of his background, but he was clearly convicted and convinced by Cuff's preaching, responded in faith and wanted to be baptized. The method adopted was that names of such people were presented to the church. Two visitors were appointed from among the notable men of the congregation, who visited the individual and reported back. On the basis of their commendation on 15th December, Wren was baptised by the pastor on 28th January 1874 and 'given the right hand of fellowship' at the Lord's Table.[22] Another significant name also appears at this time. George Cartwright was baptized on 1st April 1874 with fourteen others. He was to become Cuff's most able and loyal leader for decades to come. These converts of the pastor's early months were the gold investment that sustained a long ministry. More troubling is another name that was to cause much distress to the church. George and Jane Boggis were transferred from Downs Chapel, Clapton during this period.

Not surprisingly, the programme of three exhausting services on Sunday, which resumed again after a rest in February, told on Cuff's health. At the end of March 1873 the church abandoned the Sunday afternoon and hired the Town Hall to hold the more populous evening congregation, often turning large numbers away for lack of space. In May the church agreed to try and book the Town Hall for another twelve months.[23] They used it in this way for seven years - until the large Tabernacle was built.

Something had to be done to house the packed congregations. Providence Chapel 'had become too small for all the church members to sit at the Lord's Table together at the same time, galleries and all full.'[24] The modest Sunday School rooms, built in 1844, were also full. The teachers were turning away children. Also, in this anything but affluent area, the Town Hall hire was costing the church too much. In June 1873 the Church voted to remove the existing 'mortgage' on the Chapel and to fund 'a new spacious chapel and schools' to be opened free of debt.[25] Fundraising began in earnest. Six houses in Hackney Road, which cut off the Chapel land from its frontage, were purchased for £4000[26] and building plans were put in hand for a church to seat 2000.[27] The architect was to be Thomas Lewis Banks (1842-1920) of Finsbury Circus. Cuff had a clear idea of the building he wanted. He tells how he tried to explain his vision to Banks, then seized a pear from a passing costermonger's barrow, cut it open lengthways and held it out, saying, 'This shall be the shape of the interior and here' (indicating the stalk) 'shall be my pulpit.'[28]

The estimate of cost was an enormous £16,000, including the six houses on Hackney Road. Cuff took a cut in salary, he travelled the country fundraising. Early in 1877 he prepared and toured with a 'colloquial style' lecture about his mentor and friend C. H. Spurgeon. He used fifty lantern slides of cartoons of Spurgeon which he had seen in Spurgeon's house.[29] They had 'dissolving views' and were very popular and successful,[30] although he was criticized by some members for 'being out' so much.[31] He visited wealthy city businessmen and leading non-conformists. He persuaded Spurgeon to help and constantly urged the members to do more to raise the needed money. The church members would never have raised such a sum alone. The Building Committee had therefore to,

> earnestly, yet with confidence, commend their case to the thoughtful consideration of Christian people in all parts of the country, for they are deeply conscious that, unaided by a sympathetic public, they dare not embark in so great a work: and, therefore, they appeal to Christians of every name and denomination for help in this important undertaking.[32]

C. H. Spurgeon added his voice to the appeals:

> Mr. Cuff wishes us to report progress with regard to the Shoreditch Tabernacle, which is so greatly needed. He has obtained promises of £6000 out of £8000 which he desires to raise this year. He has heavy work before him: he has to build an immense house for a poor people, in a poor neighbourhood, and unless wealthy friends from other regions help again and again the work will hardly be accomplished. It is to be done, and will be done, the Lord being our friend's helper.[33]

In the end the whole project, including the later Lecture Hall and nearby houses, was to cost £25000.[34]

On New Year's Day 1875 the church had begun a new tradition. The pastor was in the vestry at the Chapel 'on purpose to have the pleasure of shaking hands with all the church and congregation'. Communion

Tickets, to register attendance, were handed out by a deacon. In 1878 the day was, naturally, used as a further opportunity for giving to the building fund.[35] The Annual Meeting in March is declared 'the best we have ever had'. It is clear that the leadership is united and full of faith.

I am most happy to say of Mr Cuff's work at Shoreditch that I know of nothing superior to it in its claims upon wealthy Christians. Mr Cuff has great popular gifts + attracts large numbers; he is placed among the workers & the poor, who need just such a ministry as his — This no money could purchase & if God gives the man, the least we can do is to help him to build a place to preach in. For the sake of our great population needing the gospel I beg for help for a man who preaches it with power. C. H. Spurgeon

C. H. Spurgeon's letter of support.

Cuff sums up;

> It is the joy of the Pastor's life to have men around him who are the comfort and strength of all his labour and to know that after five years and more of incessant toil in all manner of difficulties, the church and congregation are in perfect peace and much love.[36]

After these five years of Cuff's ministry, as they pressed on to build, the church was expanding with repeated scores of baptisms and new members. Some of them were young people under eighteen who, it was decided, 'were not entitled to vote at any Church Meeting'.[37] Cuff instituted an annual sermon to 'young men and maidens' at 7.00 in the morning on a Sunday in June.[38]

The church was developing an 'institutional' character: there were departments organized for children, youth and adults, for social and evangelistic work. In the summer a group of young men went on mission to Kent and Essex, holding open air services and visiting in the villages.[39] In April 1878 the third of a series of Mission Halls was opened, under one of the railway arches just up Kingsland Road. Cuff hoped for it 'to start with a trot'.[40] In June a 'Book and Magazine Depot' was added to it for the church and other Christians. It was being set up ready to move into the new Tabernacle.[41] A flavour of the commitment and energy can be seen in the church circular of 1878:

William Cuff in his prime.

> During the time of our pastor's ministry 700 persons have joined the church, an old debt of £1,200 has been cleared off, about £1,000 per annum has been raised for the current expenses of the church, including pastor's salary, Sunday-school, Dorcas Societies, Poor Funds, hire of Hall, and

incidental expenses, in addition to which two large Mission Schools, numbering about 1,000 children, have been largely supported by our congregation. We have also a Christian Mission, consisting of about 50 persons, who devote their evenings to preaching the gospel in the open-air during the summer months, and in the lodging houses and other places in the winter; also Tract Societies and other evangelistic agencies.[42]

A contemporary description of the Town Hall congregation reads,

Apparently they are not very wealthy. There are no millionaires amongst them, and there are no dashing carriages depositing fashionably-dressed ladies and West End swells at the doors of the Shoreditch Town Hall on a Sunday; and as you stand on the platform, and look at the dense mass of faces before you in the area below, and in the gallery all round, you see at once that the people are of the industrious class, for whom now an immense anxiety is professed that they should hear the gospel. The sight is imposing and impressive. There is no elaborate ritual, no ecclesiastical pomp. On the platform stands the preacher, still in his prime. He has a flashing eye, and attractive and simple manner, a voice of great sweetness and power and an earnestness that tells on that vast audience, and carries all before it. The service is as unadorned as it can possibly be. It is the old, old story that the preacher has to tell. But his heart is in his work as he beseeches men to be reconciled to God, to hold fast the Christian faith, to lead the Christian life.[43]

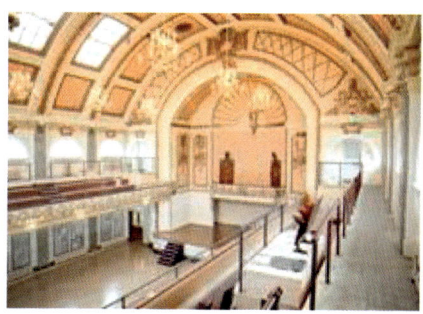

The Vestry Hall today where the church worshipped.

In the midst of this immensely fruitful activity the Cuffs suffered a deep sadness. Marianne Cuff had already given birth to five children and a sixth, William Harvey, was born in 1876. Then, at the age of 20 months, he died. Hearing the news, Spurgeon immediately wrote a touching and typically loving letter.

> Nightingale Lane, Nov. 30.
> Dear Friend, - I beseech our Lord to minister comfort both to you and your sorrowing wife. It must be a very severe stroke to you, and it is a sign that our Father loves you very much and thinks a great deal of you. I had a watch once which I allowed to lie at ease and never worried it with cleaning for I thought it worthless; but one which keeps time to a second gets wound up every night with a key which touches its inmost springs, and sometimes it gets taken to pieces—for it is worth it.
> You will have the presence of the Comforter in this trial. You are dear to me for your work's sake and also for yourself.
> May all grace abound towards you by Christ Jesus.
> Your busy friend,
> C. H. SPURGEON[44]

Marianne Cuff suffered in health after this severe bereavement, being 'very unwell for weeks past'. A wise and generous colleague, Archibald Brown of the East London Tabernacle, bought the Cuffs tickets for a much needed and medically advised holiday in Mentone in the South of France, a retreat location used many times by Spurgeon. They went during March, the deacons then sending word that they should stay two more weeks; 'Don't come home, supplies arranged for'. Letter after letter arrived with good wishes from members and reports of crowded services.[45] While the Cuffs were there, a visit to the beautiful Protestant Cemetery brought them to renewed tears and some measure of healing. Cuff writes a moving account to his people,

> To us it was a curious and tender place. We thought of a little form so precious and so beautiful, which not so long since we put into the grave and though then a thousand miles away, he seemed strangely near.[46]

Mentone in the South of France

On 2nd October 1878 for one of the final services in Providence Chapel, John Russell the former pastor came to preach from his old pulpit. The tea held in the school room was filled up 'three times'. On the 6th, after six years of ministry, William Cuff gave 31 new members 'the right hand of fellowship' and preached for the last time in the old Chapel.[47] It was then torn down. Finally the large Tabernacle began to rise on the same site, with triple doors opening onto the Hackney Road. (See map below.) Foundation stones were laid on 29th October in front of a great crowd, including 'ministers who came in such numbers'.[48] These engraved stones, re-laid, can now be seen in the outside walls of The Tab Centre.

In May 1879 the church agreed to buy the next door house, number 20 Hackney Road. A mortgage for £1000 was obtained for this purpose. A further loan of £2000 was gained for the rising building costs.[49]

Now church morning services, as well as the evenings, began in the Town Hall on October 13th. A large room under a railway arch in Thomas Street (now Cremer Street, by Hoxton Station) had been hired for the Sunday School, the weeknight services and prayer times[50] at £50 a year.[51] Weekly Monday lectures were also tried there, covering practical, political and theological topics, such as 'Some Things to be Avoided in 1879' and 'Taking Care of One's Self'. The lectures were judged successful and continued. They included an evening led by 100 members of the Church 'Choral Class', with instrumental music. Cuff also again used his famous 'dissolving views'.[52]

The Tabernacle rose up fast. The builders were 'busy as bees' and hoped that it would be ready in October. The interior measured 120ft by 80ft with a gallery on three sides, a platform covering the baptistry and the pulpit raised and central.[53] It is not surprising that in Shoreditch, with scores of able craftsmen and women, members of the church made the furniture and other items under the instruction of 'The Furnishing Committee'. A wood turner and a polisher worked for nothing.[54]

Mission work continued apace, led by energetic teams of evangelists and visitors. The Kingsland Road Mission (not directly run from, but supported by the church) reports,

> two hundred families are regularly visited, hundreds of visits paid and thousands of tracts distributed... ... and above all some souls won to faith Christ.[55]

The pastor and elders attempted to keep on top of the pastoral work of the exploding congregation. They surveyed the list of members every month. Those not attending communion were named at Members' Meetings and 'withdrawn from'. To record their presence, members had to put their 'communion tickets' in the plate on Sunday, along with their offerings. All monetary gifts were properly recorded. But one week there were 20 blanks in the record.

> One deacon scratched his head, another took some snuff, and a third was about to move a resolution, when a fourth said,
> 'Brethren, the dear people only forgot it', and then they all agreed it was a bad week.[56]

An odd 'bad week' would not stop the advance. Soon Shoreditch Tabernacle was ready for the congregation to move in.

But ominously large sums had recently been borrowed to pay the builders.

Internal view of Cuff's Tabernacle

Chapter 5

The New Tabernacle

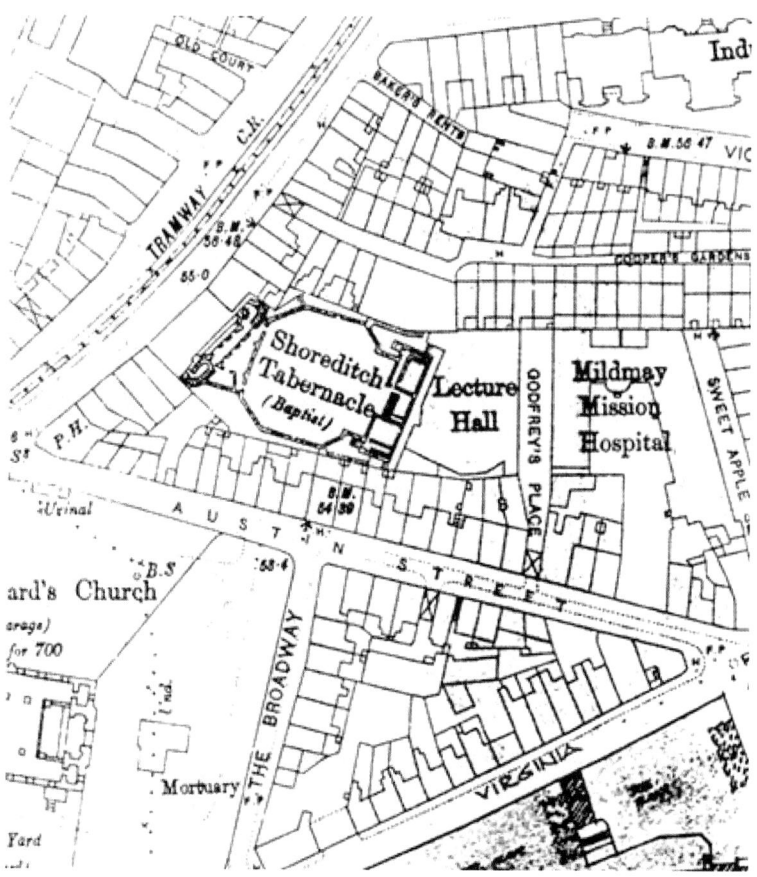

Detail from the 1894 Ordnance Survey map.

At eight in the morning on Tuesday, 11th November, 1879 William Cuff stood up to lead the very first prayer in Shoreditch Tabernacle at a public service. 'The acoustic properties proved well-nigh perfect.'[57] Dr. Alexander Maclaren, a well-known Baptist preacher, came from Manchester to preach at noon and the place was 'crowded in every part, standing spaces included.'[58] Cuff records,

Young and old wept and sang alike. Minister and people were overwhelmed, and the glory of the Lord seemed to fill His House as of old... ... the whole assembly seemed baptized in the spirit and power of prayer.[59]

Afterwards a Public Luncheon was laid on for 400 in the Town Hall at 5/- a seat. Its galleries opened to the public at 2.30, so anyone could get in 'free of all charge' to hear the M.P. for Hackney and other speakers. Three weeks of special services followed, including meetings for young people and children. It all ended with a tea in the Town Hall and a Public Thanksgiving Service in the Tabernacle on Monday, December 1st 1879. Notable visitors and preachers came and took part including Rev. Joseph Parker of the City Temple and Dr. Thomas Barnardo, founder of the famous children's homes.[60] On the first Sunday evening the former pastor, Rev John Russell, led Communion in the Tabernacle 'to which nearly 1000 communicants attended' with the gallery well filled with spectators.[61]

The Sunday congregations moved back from the Town Hall to the Tabernacle. The new place was full and the varied work of the church

Drawing from Walker, *East London*, p.74

went on unhindered. On Sunday nights particularly they were 'pestered for room'.[62] In a full account of the first evening meeting during that week, the *Shoreditch Observer* tells how Cuff went to the front and was 'met with a very enthusiastic reception'. The crowds cheered loudly and repeatedly as he named many individuals and the actual sums they donated to the cause. This turned into another fundraising opportunity; Cuff never missed one. He specified the 'deficiency' of £5000 and announced a revised figure of £2500 he hoped to raise by the end of the celebration weeks.[63]

In the end the target was missed by a large margin; the debt remained and the church was continually in financial need. Among other means, they raised further funds with a Bazaar (April 1880), a concert by Mr. Spurgeon's Orphan Boys (Good Friday) and another with Handbell Ringers (May). In a sign of continuing difficulty the Deacons 'resolved that all the sittings in the new building be let at a certain sum per quarter' with the amount yet to be decided upon.[64]

A depressing and shocking aspect of the whole project is recorded by Cuff.

> But soon after the Tab was opened there came a rude awakening, at least for me. All the accounts had to be audited and we found there was a debt of some £8000 on the building. Somebody had not been straight. It was all traced, and the guilty found out. I was broken-hearted and ill, and compelled to go away and rest. I came back and tackled it all again, and grappled with the huge debt. Our dear people stood by me, and tackled it too, with brave hearts. Little by little we got the debt down, but still it was heavy and crippled us in everything.[65]

'The guilty' is never named in any record we have, but Evans is right to conclude that it was George Boggis, the financial secretary of the building committee.[66] He was a Public Accountant by profession. He must have known what was happening. Large sums of money were passing through his hands and he may have misused the funds, although nothing is recorded. George and his wife Jane had transferred their membership from Downs Chapel, Clapton in March 1873. He was a very useful man, elected deacon the following February. He was respected and trusted, active and creative. Cuff called him 'our indefatigable friend'.[67] Boggis was soon involved in the funding of the new Tabernacle and became the financial secretary to the building committee. He gave a long spiritually framed report on the situation, with a further appeal, to a large public meeting in the Town Hall in March 1877.[68]

The Tabernacle was built, but six months afterwards the truth emerged. There was consternation among the elders and deacons. In May 1880 Hatton resigned as an elder. A letter from a member, Mr Hayes, to Cuff was read out to the church along with his reply. Sawell, one of the deacons, stated he 'could not endorse some of the statements in the pastor's letter' and immediately announced his resignation. A small group agreed with him and voted against accepting Cuff's response.[69] The deacons did not have a meeting for nine months.

In June Boggis proposed a new mortgage of £4000 to pay the builder. In July one deacon, Mr Hannaford, called for fresh leadership elections immediately, probably to replace those not presently functioning. He refused to answer the Pastor's questions from the chair and the meeting voted that he 'not be heard'.[70] More money was borrowed and more leaders resigned, or expressed a wish to do so. Cuff lost three elders by resignation during that year. One of them, Mr Peppiatt, a loyal elder, was absent from the church for no stated reason. He was visited and 'commended for prayer' to the church.[71] The elders and deacons were clearly in disarray. Cuff was indeed 'broken-hearted'.

Finally it all came to a head. After eighteen months delay Boggis had still not prepared accounts of the building fund. In Feb 1881 he had been 'unable to arrange an appointment to meet with the auditors.' Sawell, now on the back benches, asked when this would be done and the answer was vague: 'as early as possible'. The church was divided. Some wanted independent auditors and the accounts immediately published. Others wished to give Boggis more time and this was agreed.[72] The deacons and elders repeatedly requested all the books and accounts while Boggis stalled for over two years. In the end the auditors found a building fund deficit of £8000.

Cuff was ill and off work for three months in 1883 for no stated reason. The architect, Lewis Banks, repeatedly put in his final bill for £161 and had no response from Boggis. In the end Cuff offered him £50 as a personal payment to settle the bill, which he refused. In 1886 he wrote an aggrieved letter detailing work for which he had not been paid and demanding settlement. The deacons at first ignored him. Then they settled the matter with a payment of £106.[73]

Severe relational damage in the church is visible in the records. So is the loss, over several years, of significant previously loyal and able leaders. In January 1884 five more elders resigned.[74] The following May Cuff told the church that as a whole they were still £10,000 in debt. Boggis finally resigned as a deacon at the end of 1883 without the usual vote of thanks, often warmly effusive.[75] George and Jane Boggis themselves were damaged by all this and were removed from membership in December 1885, for 'walking inconsistently'.[76] The church lost touch with them soon afterwards.

Strangely, while this sad tale unfolded, there were still multiple baptisms and scores of people joining the church, now worshipping in the new building. A congregation of up to 2000 on Sundays still enjoyed Cuff's direct and godly preaching. Even if they knew of the tensions among the core of the church, they continued supporting Cuff and his remaining leaders in their apparently uncondemning attitude to those who had let them down so badly. There is not a word of personal criticism of Boggis, or anyone else, in the records. The harmonious spirit of the church recovered and some new, able elders and deacons were soon elected.

One of these was George Cartwright, brought to Christ and baptized by Cuff ten years before. In 1884 Cartwright, recently elected a deacon, became the church secretary.[77] He lived at 192, Barnet Grove, Hackney, ten minutes' walk from the church, and a similar distance from the Cuffs in Cambridge Heath. He ran a grocer's shop,[78] one of many such successful tradesmen in the congregation. He applied his considerable business and personal skills to the great benefit of the church. He was to be Cuff's loyal and capable 'armour bearer' for the rest of his long ministry. A new period had begun.

George Cartwright in later life

Chapter 6

A Spiritual Community with Dinners

The culture of the church was widely inclusive. An authoritative contemporary account notes that in this church 'the working class prevails, together with that proportion of the lower middle which is almost indistinguishable from the upper working class.'[1] However, inclusive did not mean gender equality. As was the general custom, only men voted at church meetings[2] and only men were eligible to be deacons or elders. Early in Cuff's ministry there was a complaint because he and the deacons had permitted 'a lady to lead the singing'. No debate was allowed and Miss Sarah Lucas was publicly thanked by Cuff 'for having kindly led the singing for some time past'.[3] On only one occasion was a woman appointed as a 'messenger' to visit a prospective couple for membership - along with her husband of course.

There are continual references in the record to 'the working man and his wife', to 'young men and maidens' or 'the young folks'. There was the deliberate encouragement of young children and families. The children's teachers are regularly honoured and applauded. Cuff's wittily expressed policy on mothers with babies says that 'we very much wish them to come to chapel and mission hall services'. They should sit as near the door as possible so that 'should the preacher frighten the baby, the mother might take it out without disturbing the preacher, or what is more, the congregation'.[4] Many of the hard-pressed people came late to services. Cuff points out firmly that the services are *not* at 11.15 a.m. and 6.45 p.m. They should be in their places five minutes early, so that worship can begin solemnly with prayer and 'a burst of united song'.[5]

Wide appeal is one thing, but at the same time the church was a well-defined community. Cuff says,

> A church if true to its divine appointment is a *spiritual community,* a voluntary association of saved and sanctified souls. Our membership is definitely based on this idea.[6]

They may have been inclusive at the table ('open communion'), but the members were expected to be baptized as believers ('closed membership'). They were not only spiritually committed, they were eager to take part in the management of the church, especially after the crisis of 1880. There are hints about conflict and over-zealous speaking at Church Members business meetings. Large numbers came, more than for prayer meetings, which grieved Cuff.[7] The elders sought to disciple the lax and also to keep the large membership numbers realistic. Those who moved away, or who did not come to worship, were regularly removed from the roll, sometimes in very large groups.[8]

The purpose of the church was first of all to preach and witness to the gospel of Christ and to see people come to faith in him. During the summer of 1880 a large team organised Open Air Meetings in nine locations: five on a Sunday and four more during the week, as well as 24 meetings run at the Brick Lane mission. Much was made, in the mission centres as well as the church, of those who were converted to Christ and baptised. The testimony of a young man seeking membership is recorded and concludes;

> Between seven and eight o'clock in the evening of January 23rd, 1878, I passed out of the darkness of the past into the light and blessedness of a clear hope... ... happy and thankful to God for his gracious deliverance. If I am asked what Christ has done for me, I answer - he fulfilled the law, died, rose, and now makes intercession for me at God the Father's right hand. All my trust is stayed on him and I know I shall never be ashamed, because he has said so.[9]

William Fullerton and J. Manton Smith

In September 1881 William Fullerton and J. Manton Smith of Spurgeon's College Society of Evangelists held a series of meetings in Shoreditch, many in the Tabernacle. Large crowds heard the evangelists preach and Manton Smith sang and played the cornet. On the Sunday afternoons nearly three thousand men filled the church. Cuff said, 'It is a splendid sight to see so many skilled mechanics together.' There were meetings for women only too. Each night every seat was taken and many remained after the services for prayer and counselling. They were assisted on occasions by Vernon J. Charlesworth, who Spurgeon had appointed as Master of his boy's Orphanage and supported by Joseph Passmore, Spurgeon's friend, deacon and publisher Cuff describes these gatherings in a breathless letter from the church during the meetings.

> My dear Mr. Spurgeon,
> The 'Song Service' last night was an *unbounded success*. The place was suffocatingly full, and there were literally hundreds who strove about the doors, and then at the gates, pleading in vain to get in. Our two beloved brethren were both at their very best, and did exceedingly well, the Lord being with them. These Song Services of Mr. Charlesworth are unique in interest and power. They add vastly to the rest of the work. There is so much gospel in them, put in a novel, taking, yet proper manner. They must do good. Fancy four thousand people of all sorts moved by them on a Saturday night in a district so busy as this! Let the fact tell their power. Sceptics and Christians alike came last night. We know the people, and therefore write with certainty. Mr. Passmore and Mr. Charlesworth were here last night; and they can testify to what I tell you. In the mouth of two or three witnesses every word shall be established. We had a service this morning at seven o'clock. There was a very large gathering, and the two dear fellows were here in good time. They were again at their best, and it was the best service we have yet held. The Tabernacle seemed full of holy power. The Lord was here. I hope these things will cheer your heart in the midst; of all you have to try your faith and hope. It was something for you to take *me* into the College, and fit me for the ministry. It was no small matter for the Lord to move his people to give money to build this house, but now he has given to you to set in motion such a work as Fullerton and Smith are doing, not only here, but everywhere they go. I am glad they come from the dear old College. May the good Lord send more

men to the College who will step out of old ruts, and be men of originality and real power! 2.30 p.m. - A crowded house at 11, and a word of much power from Mr. Fullerton. The men are now crowding in for their service. Oh, for power! I am now stopped by a man who enters to tell me an infidel was here at this morning, and so touched was he that he has just come into the Tabernacle, and vows to a friend that by God's help he will seek Christ. We are going specially to pray for him. What wonders does the old gospel achieve! I will continue by-and-by. These are scraps ... Afternoon service for men just now over. If it be possible the place was more crammed than last Sunday afternoon, and there was £1-13s more in the offering. Last Sunday they gave £7. Mr. Smith preached, Mr. Fullerton read, and I prayed. What a sight! This huge place crowded with men of every class and condition! I am contented to leave all results with God, for I know he will save many through his word.[10]

The church also engaged deeply with the society round about. There was a blatant current of political activism in the church. The Disraeli Government was accused of 'Imperialism' by Cuff in 1879 and he was 'impertinent enough to say that he trusted that when the next general election came every man in that house at least would do his duty. (Great applause)'[11] Unashamed, he later wrote, 'vote for Liberalism, as against Toryism'.[12] They did so. The 1880 victory of Gladstone, 'a conscientious and intensely honest man', was celebrated by a people 'sick of the lying and trickery' of the Tories.[13] Financial needs of local people were also addressed. A Building Society was set up, with Cuff as the deputy chair, 'mainly for the benefit of our own friends' but also for anyone who needed financial help. Cuff urges, 'Let every young man .... *begin at once to get a house of his own.*'[14]

One of the most creative benevolent enterprises set up at this time was the Christmas Dinner provision. Many churches in poor districts offered such charity, but every secular account of Shoreditch Baptists at this time mentions the dinners and Cuff's butchering skills from his former profession. Funds were raised annually for the purpose. Cuff organized the sides of beef from local shops, personally selected the cuts of meat, prepared the joints and supervised the distribution.[15] The practice was continued during his absence in Australasia in December 1902. Rightly proud of this work, Cuff explained,

> [I]f I had been at home on Christmas Eve, instead of being in

Invercargill, I should have cut up two tons of beef into little pieces, weighing from four to twelve pounds each. These we distribute to the very poor, with bread, groceries, etc., that they may have a good solid Christmas dinner in their own places. We never give a public feed, because I feel strongly that that only pauperises and degrades the poor. We do all in our power to cultivate home life. The poor have not suffered through my absence in the colonies, for my eldest daughter and the deacons have done what I should have done.[16]

A family sitting down to a hearty meal at Christmas, perhaps the first for a long time, would know gratefully that the Baptist Pastor's hands had cut the meat. A better marketing strategy for a church in this area could hardly be invented.

Education and self-improvement were high on the agenda. The Book Depot was moved into the Tabernacle under the able hand of J. Everett, one of the elders. He also wrote substantial portions of the church magazine, an educational as much as a spiritual publication. Number 20 Hackney Road, on the left side of the church, had been bought with a mortgage of £1000.[17] The tenants were willing to move out. Job Wren, baptized by Cuff in January 1874, had become Chapel Keeper and this house on the church frontage became the Jobs' home. The front room was refitted as a bookshop, which he managed.[18] It provided good literature, both Christian and secular, books and periodicals.[19]

Leisure trips out of the city, especially to the seaside, featured in the annual programme of the church and the mission schools. Cheaply priced, they made good use of the new and exciting railways recently laid into the heart of London. The local papers saw the good works and godly influence of the church as leading to 'an increase in sobriety and pure living, a dispersion of mental gloom and inward unrest, and a diminution of the pauperism and crime which afflict the community.'[20]

Cuff was a personable and credible leader. He won substantial help from other churches and business people to support him in the work. Heath Street Baptist, Hampstead, in a very different area with a wealthy congregation, repeatedly contributed to the endless financial needs of the church. Friends from that area gave the seed money to build the Tabernacle.[21] Their pastor, William Brock became an ally and friend to Cuff and they often exchanged pulpits. The gratitude of the church to Brock and the generosity of his people at Hampstead is mentioned a number of times in the records.

A local chemist William Fox was another faithful friend. With his sons C. E. and R. W. Fox he had a business in Bethnal Green Road and later they had other chemist shops.[22] Fox was not a member of the Tabernacle, but he was deeply committed to Cuff and his church. Cuff says he baptized ten of his, or perhaps his sons' children. The father and sons gave £100 each to the heavy Tabernacle debt at 'the most critical time in our history'.[23] Fox also helped to set up and fund the Kingsland Road mission and supported the Brick Lane Mission (later at Gibraltar Walk), both supervised by the Tabernacle.

WILLIAM FOX,
Wholesale and Retail Chemist
SUPPLIES
BARYTES, CHLORATE, POTASH,
PHOSPHORUS, STRONTIA
AND OTHER CHEMICALS
Pure and Commercial, at
Market Prices

Even more significant than his financial backing was his vision to care for the many Mission workers and Sunday School teachers attached to the Tabernacle. He arranged a quarterly tea and conference for all of them in his large house in Upper Clapton, simply to give them a good time, what we would now call 'bonding'. This support meeting was continued by his sons, in total for 30 years 'without a break'. Cuff's conclusion is that it was,

> ... the secret of keeping our workers in close touch with one another, and a continued inspiration to them in all the missions. It is not possible to tabulate all that these meetings have done for the workers and missions over the years.[24]

For much of the period until the mid-90s Shoreditch Tabernacle had the largest membership and congregation north of the Thames, matched only by The East London Tabernacle and Westbourne Park, Paddington. It was still usual for Baptist churches to rent pews to regular worshippers, but this main source of income had been abandoned at Shoreditch in 1858. Walker's description of a service he attended in 1896 reads,

> Through the open doors of Mr Cuff's great Tabernacle, throngs of the better class of well-dressed working people are passing and take their seats. There are no rented seats in the spacious

building; all comers alike are welcomed, and before service begins a congregation of some three thousand has assembled. The preacher occupies a pulpit platform, with a large and competent choir on a gallery behind him. The singing is supported (not led) by the organ. From the choir gallery behind the preacher the congregation presents an impressive scene. The majority are young people, in the first flower of their age, for Mr Cuff is a favourite with the young, as the overflowing Sunday schools adjoining attest. Yet the opening prayer with its deeply-sympathetic petitions for the aged and the sorrowing, give full assurance of a large-hearted pastorate for old and young alike. The sermon has for its high aim the salvation, sanctification and full equipment of man for the service of God and his fellow-men.

Cuff is proud to claim that the 'Tabernacle services are among the brightest in London', even though the task of the preacher is a solemn one and 'the people not seldom laugh and cry by turns.'[25]

The view from the pulpit in the Tabernacle.

Chapter 7

Children and the School Room

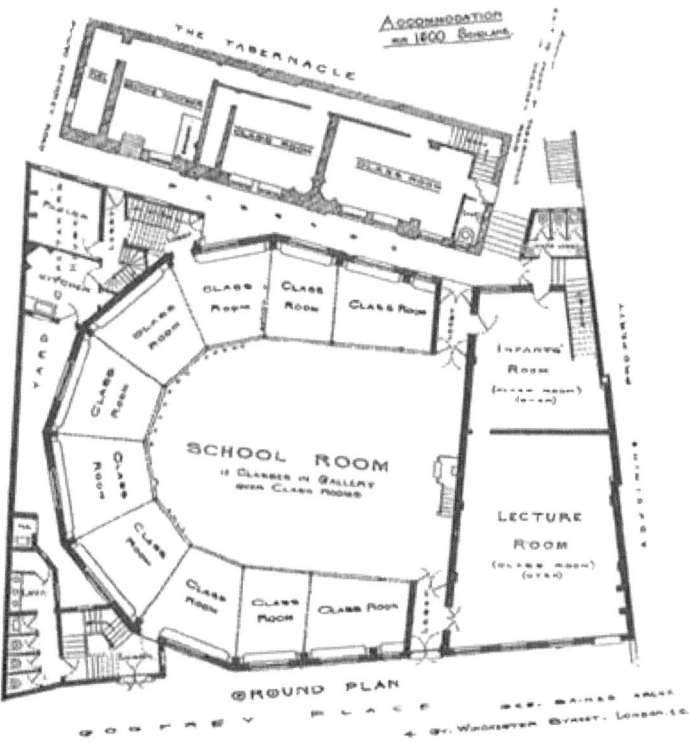

Architect's plan of the School Room

The next project of the church had always been in mind. It was to create 'school buildings', now called 'The Tab Centre', a rare building of its type and Grade II listed in 2002. It was desperately needed. The sheer numbers of children wanting to attend was enormous. Sunday schools in Shoreditch were;

> full to overflowing; the children sit on the floor in double rows around their teachers; and in sheer despair, the superintendent closes his books, while he assures the crowd of applicants out-of-doors that he can receive no more until new schools are erected.[1]

Land behind the Tabernacle facing Godfrey Place, had already been obtained for this purpose.[2] The few small houses were demolished and work began. Foundation stones were laid on 24th February, 1890. They are still to be seen in walls in Godfrey Place. The opening finally took place in July 1891. It could hardly be seen from the outside, being hemmed in by surrounding buildings, but it is described as 'a beautiful octagonal school building, with conical roof, clerestory, gallery, central hall, and separate bays cut off for classes,... ... one of the most notable and best equipped edifices for its purpose in the kingdom.'[3]

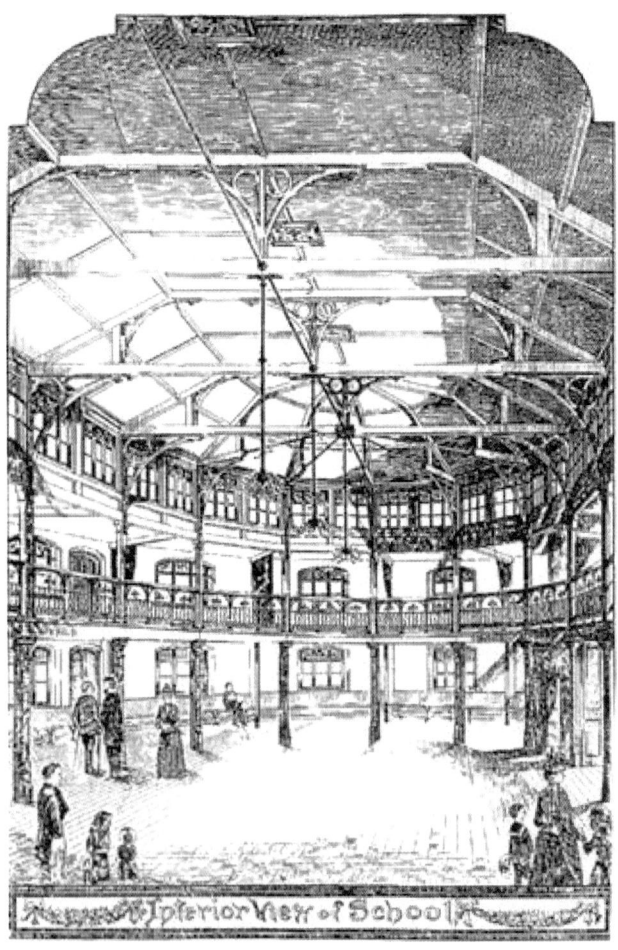

It still stands and you can visit and compare its present condition with a description in The *Baptist Handbook* for 1890.

> These schools are about to be erected in the rear of Shoreditch Tabernacle, and it is expected they will be opened in July next. The total estimated cost of the scheme is £4,200. The building will consist of a large central school-room, fifty feet by thirty-five feet, with ten large class rooms ranged round it in a horseshoe shape, as shown on plan, shut off from it by means of revolving wood shutters and having wickets therein, and divided from each other by panelled partitions, which can be pushed up in sections against the walls, so as to throw the whole space on the ground floor into one large room, sixty-five feet by sixty-five feet. Above the side class rooms is a gallery which will accommodate twelve class-rooms, and open to the central schoolroom. This will be lighted by clerestory lights over the flat roofs of the gallery which will be formed on iron joists and concrete finished with Seyssel asphalte. The clerestory windows will open for ventilation.
>
> In addition to these rooms there will be an infants' classroom, twenty feet by twenty-one feet, a lecture room, twenty-five feet by thirty-two feet, and two large class rooms over these. All the necessary lavatories and offices are also provided; and a caretaker's house. Three spacious fireproof staircases are provided from the upper floor, and six wide doorways for exit, all of which will open outwards.
>
> The floor will be of wood blocks on solid concrete. The joinery will be varnished. The schools will be well heated and ventilated, and the sanitary arrangements will be complete. There will be accommodation for about 1,500 scholars.
>
> The architect is Mr George Baines, 4 Great Winchester Street, London EC.[4]

The central purpose of the building was declared in capital letters with verses from Matthew 18.14 and 19.14 painted round the gallery;

> 'It is not the will of your Father which is in heaven that one of these little ones should perish... Suffer little children and forbid them not to come unto me: for of such is the kingdom of heaven.'

The deacons thanked William Perkins, a member and the grandson of one of the church founders, 'for having the gallery front written with texts'. With an interest in church furnishing and décor through the family trimming makers' business, Perkins had paid for the work to be done.⁵ (See further p. 113)

Eleanore (1847-1924) and William Perkins (1843-1924)

A brief, but serious crisis occurred in 1893. Cuff, now 53, was invited to be the pastor of one of the noblest Baptist churches in the country, Broadmead Bristol, founded in 1640. It was a prestigious post and would have been a very good move. But the church was horrified. When Cuff told the deacons, with one voice they pleaded with him to stay, acknowledging that they 'must improve his position here "financially"'. Urgent meetings were arranged with the Elders. Cuff declined to give an answer till he had visited Bristol. It is not clear if he went. A special Members Meeting was called on Sunday March 19th which unanimously resolved to write to 'our beloved Pastor', and urge him that 'nothing may transpire to sever the close connection of twenty years standing' and that he would complete his life's work 'by remaining in our midst.' A deputation of representatives was appointed to go to him and urge this resolution.[6]

Nothing more is heard of the proposed move, but in May the church voted to increase Cuff's stipend by £100.[7] Many others in the area were also relieved. James Hewetson, a member of the supportive Hampstead Church, wrote to Cartwright

> May a double blessing on his honoured ministry attend this determination of Mr Cuff to labour on amongst his own children in the faith, cheered as he is and will be, by the hearty practical good will and prayers of friends, not only at the Tabernacle but at Hampstead and elsewhere.[8]

Toward the turn of the century the area around the church was gradually changing. These changes signalled the end of the church as it had been. Social work became more and more important. Cuff's preaching was still popular, but mission and social work occupied the church, which served an enormous number of people. The Sunday school in the new building had 1300 children in 1898.[9] There were 300 workers, visiting, preaching and teaching the poorest people, many of them based on missions located in the wider area, some in former churches of other denominations others meeting in local school buildings.

They were sustained by an increasingly working class membership.[10] Though not all at the same time and not all uniquely supported by the Tabernacle, missions had begun at: Bethel Chapel, a former Baptist church in Austin Street/Virginia Row, Kingsland Road Hall, Union Crescent, Gibraltar Walk (the largest), Wellington Street, Vincent Street, Shacklewell Street, Hoxton House (Friends Meeting) in Old Castle Street, Collingwood Street, Hope Mission in Haggerston and Shap Street.[11]

The mission at Shap Street (between Ormsby Street and Appleby Street) met in a board school building only a mile from the Tabernacle. It served over 300 children on Sundays in three 'schools', morning, afternoon and evening. At their annual 'Festival' held at the Tabernacle in January 1899, 150 children aged over twelve were present on the Wednesday and 350 under twelve on the Friday. The loyal Job Wren appears too. He was 'very kind and obliging, thus adding to the success of the evenings', and he contributed to the Festival in 1903 with a lantern entertainment and the school paid for limes and gas to light his show.[12] A dedicated staff of teachers, some of them teenagers who rose through the classes, assisted a group of leaders and officers in teaching and visiting the families.

Other activities initiated by Shap Street mission included a Dorcas Society (providing clothes for poor families), a Benevolent Society, Bible classes, preparation for Scripture Examinations and Open Air services. For a number of years these were held at the corner of Pearson Street and Kingsland Road. The Country Homes scheme paid for selected children to go for two weeks holiday out of London. One year, under financial constraint the teachers agreed to pay only half the cost, but having visited one family 'in very poor circumstances' and unable to pay their share, the teachers agreed to pay all.[13]

In spite of all the good children's work there was opposition, from the local Anglican parish church in particular. In one report numbers suffered 'through teachers at the Church school telling scholars not to go to the Chapel School'. In a different way, trouble at the school gates was dealt with by appointing a 'gatekeeper' to refuse the unruly after 'Mr Lane said he had a new silk hat spoiled with a stone'.[14]

These hours of service and effort was often crowned with success as children made a response of faith. At one teachers meeting the 'conversion' of five children was reported, at another four had decided for Christ and 'this was received with praise and thanksgiving by all present'.

However, able church leaders were moving out as Shoreditch evolved into a commercial district. Cuff was burdened by the enormity of the social need. The area known as 'Old Nichol', a long stone's throw from the Tabernacle, had been desperately poor and deprived for decades. One account describes the conditions of the inhabitants as,

> nothing but one painful and monotonous round of vice, filth, and poverty, huddled in dark cellars, ruined garrets, bare and blackened rooms, reeking with disease and death, and without the means for the most ordinary observations of decency or cleanliness.[15]

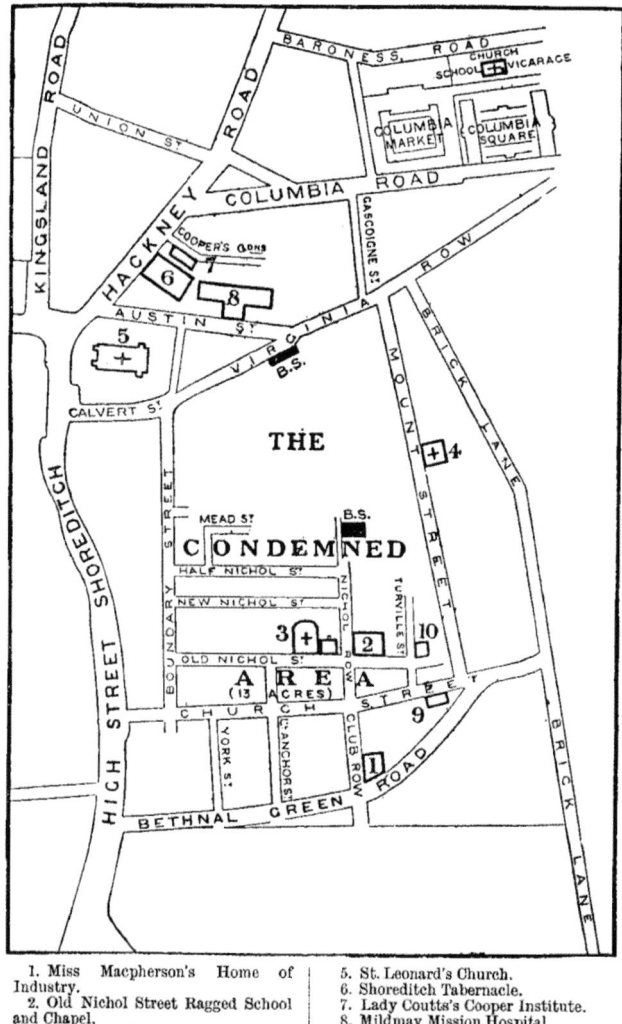

1. Miss Macpherson's Home of Industry.
2. Old Nichol Street Ragged School and Chapel.
3. The Rev. Osborne Jay's Church and Lodging-House.
4. St. Philip's Church.
5. St. Leonard's Church.
6. Shoreditch Tabernacle.
7. Lady Coutts's Cooper Institute.
8. Mildmay Mission Hospital.
9. Mildmay Lodging-House.
10. Mildmay Mission Rooms.

The 'Old Nichol' from Walker, p. 93

It was finally cleared by the London County Council in 1891 and rebuilt as the Boundary Estate, the first purpose built 'council estate', which still stands. About the wider district, Cuff explains that in the latter part of the 19th century

> there were many streets with nothing but dwelling houses in

them, and these were occupied by well-to-do people. Now they are full of offices of business places ... the well-to-do people are all gone to live elsewhere.[16]

The congregation honoured Cuff greatly and his achievements were widely recognized. He was on the Baptist Union Council, elected President of the London Baptist Association in 1894 and President of the Baptist Union in 1900. Part of the wider work he did was in connection with a controversial series of Education Acts.

Cuff had been elected to the London School Board for Hackney district in 1888 and served three years, advocating the teaching of the Bible in schools.[17] Most dissenters were supporters of the School Boards and of non-denominational Bible education in schools.[18] The Act which passed in 1902 however, was bitterly opposed by non-conformists, especially Baptists, because it gave Government funding to Anglican and Catholic schools. Seen by Baptists as an 'unjust tax', it led to imprisonment for many who refused to pay their council rates for this reason. Together with his church, Cuff fiercely opposed it. He said, 'Thousands of nonconformists will never pay the rate if the Act remains as it is. They are more than ever resolved to fight it to the end.'[19] During his visit to Australasia he was questioned several times about his views.

But this is the lively story of the next chapter.

Chapter 8

The Sweet Air of Hackney Road

After 30 years at Shoreditch the energy of Cuff's early ministry was fading. So also was his health. The weekly ministry and the church were affected. After a four year period of increasing ill-health with 'dyspepsia', in order 'to avert a complete collapse', the church generously agreed in 1902 to release him, with his wife, for a long journey to Australia and New Zealand. By the generosity of his friend the banker George Ackland they sailed in September in the *Omrah*, returning in February 1903. The trip was a complete success. Cuff came back 'a bronzed and cheery giant', invigorated after an immensely enjoyable time.

> After all our wanderings we arrived at home, sweet home! safe and sound. Rest and change had done wonders for our health; we were rested in body and mind; shattered nerves were strung up once more while that miserable dyspepsia was left in the breezes of the sea or on the crests of the waves, we fondly hope never to return. We felt young again and fit for the work that awaited us amongst the toiling masses and the poor of Shoreditch.[1]

THE REV. WILLIAM CUFF.

HIS IMPRESSIONS OF AUSTRALIA.

The eminent Baptist London divine, the Rev. William Cuff, who arrived in October last, is returning home by the mail steamer Omrah, which called at Largs Bay on Thursday. He immediately recognised the interviewer who interrogated him on the Education Bill and kindred topics on his arrival. "I have been a long way since I saw you last," he said.

Have your impressions of Australia reached your anticipations? asked our representative.

"Very far beyond that," was the reply.

Equally important, the church had continued its demanding programme, even without his ministry and leadership. This speaks well for the strength and ability of the members and leaders of that time. At the celebration on Thursday April 2nd, marking the Cuff's return, the *Baptist Times* reporter who was present wrote,

> Prior to the Reception I found my way to the deacons' vestry, and had a brief chat with Mr. G. Cartwright, the secretary of the Church and Mr. Cuff.'s right-hand man. He told me that during Mr. Cuff's absence the congregations had been well maintained, and all the work of the Church had gone on as usual. The services for the last six or seven Sundays had been conducted by Mr Gange, whose ministrations had been greatly enjoyed, and his labours, as well as those of Dr Macgregor and other friends, had been owned and blessed of God.

Cartwright as 'the pastor's chief armour-bearer' chaired the later meeting in the Tabernacle and when he rose 'with radiant face, at his honoured post, a volley of greetings rang out in heartfelt appreciation of a great work nobly done.'[2]

That day the church, 'throbbing in every heart with faith, hope and love, welcomed back its pastor with a torrent of affection, and spread around his worthy wife a garland of goodwill.' After a two hour reception in the Schoolroom, during which Mr and Mrs Cuff shook hands with 1000 people, they all adjourned to the chapel which was packed out.

> [T]he deacons filed on to the platform, followed by Mrs. Cuff and the pastor. Instantly the great audience sprang to its feet, and a scene of wild enthusiasm ensued and lasted for some moments. The people cheered, and stamped, and waved handkerchiefs and hymn-sheets, while Mr. Cuff stood there, his strong face working with emotion and with the tears in his eyes.[3]

Cartwright's speech touched the same notes of thanks and appreciation for the way that the church had been blessed in Cuff's absence.

> You will be glad to know, too, dear pastor, that in your absence the great Shepherd of the Church has been good to us as a Church and people, and has kept us together in peace and unity. As officers of the Church we are glad to hand back the responsibility of the service and work of the Church to your

hands; but we want to testify that our God has been good to us (cheers) that in the ministry He has led the flock into green pastures and beside the still waters; and, blessed be His name, He has not left us without proof that the Word preached has been blessed to the salvation of some precious souls. And He has also silenced the croakers. Some there were who said, 'Ah! Now we shall see the congregations diminish, the Church scattered, the funds all go wrong.' But we have to bear our testimony to the facts; that from the highest work to the lowest' if there be any high or low in God's work, everything has gone well. Our congregations have kept up, our finances also, our week-night services have increased, our prayer-meetings have been blessed times of power, and, as a Church and people, we were never in a better spirit to go on with the work of the Lord, and to extend the work of the Church. We take this, dear pastor, as a proof of the sterling character of the work you have done here for the past thirty years, and we trust you will get great encouragement to go forward as you see your work has not been in vain in the Lord. Our wish and prayer for you is that you may be kept well and strong, and that God may bless you in your work here for many years to come. (Cheers.)

After the speeches of welcome and thanks, Cuff stood to speak to the congregation. It was some minutes before the cheering subsided and he could be heard. He was full of gratitude to God for his goodness and mercy on their 40,000 mile journey. Equally he recognised the way the church had been kept and united in love during his absence

> He was glad to be in their midst once more, speaking in the building that was to him the most sacred place on earth. 'Not half-dead, as we have been,' he cried, in tones that rang through the Tabernacle, 'but alive from head to foot, and ready to preach the Gospel which has so often been the power of God unto salvation within these walls.' There was no place like home, and there were no people like his own people. And no words could express his joy to find that they were not tired of him, but were glad to have him back.

It was an opportunity for teasing humour too as he recalled the places they had seen.

> He convulsed the audience with laughter when he said that he

had breathed the fiery breath of the desert in the Red Sea, and the fresh, cool breezes of the Pacific and the bracing air of the mountains in New Zealand, but there was no atmosphere anywhere so sweet as that of the Hackney Road[4]

And what did the people think of all this? The reporter concludes,

> They give you good measure, pressed down and running over, at Shoreditch Tabernacle, and yet people are not satisfied. As I passed out, close on eleven o'clock, I heard enthusiastic Tabernaclers wishing the meeting had lasted two hours longer! There is something invigorating in the air of Hackney!

By 1903 numbers on Sunday had decreased, with 546 in the morning and 1220 in the evening.[5] Attendance did not reflect the membership which stood at 900 in the same year. Cuff had returned after his long holiday healthy and renewed and the church entered a short period of recovery. It was still a formidable force in the area. For example the oldest mission agency, the House to House Visiting Agency continued unhindered.

> No less than eight hundred families are visited every Sunday. At each house a copy of the week's issue of the Religious Tract Society's Friendly Greetings is left, this being changed for a new one on the Sunday following. The people eagerly receive this attractive reading, illustrated with fine pictures. Twenty thousand copies are needed yearly; and such an outlay and distribution seems to be the most ready way of directly introducing the Gospel into homes which might otherwise remain ignorant about the good news or glad tidings.[6]

The place of women in the church was gradually changing. In a Deacons' Meeting in 1913 it was 'unanimously agreed' that 'Lady Messengers' should be appointed to visit prospective 'lady members' and this was done at a subsequent church meeting.[7]

A serious problem was developing with the Tabernacle fabric. Erected speedily and with an eye to minimizing costs, it was deteriorating after only 25 years. By 1904 it needed urgent renovation inside and out. The surveyor was of the opinion 'that the work must not be delayed, but should be put in hand at once'. It was reported;

> Water comes through the roof and drops on the people during

rain; the brick-work of the walls needs to be pointed; while the interior requires to be thoroughly cleaned or renovated. As the expense of doing what is needed will not cost less than £2,000, the matter really becomes a serious crisis to a congregation which is largely made up of working people. 'I am in distress about it, and know not what we shall do,' said the pastor to a company of his friends, after he had heard the particulars. 'A debt will cripple us again just when our best work was never better.'

The members did respond. 'Hundreds of men attending Mr. Cuff's ministry ... pledged themselves to do what was possible.' But the financial resources of the nominal 900 church members were increasingly limited. At a memorable church meeting where the repairs and renovation came up for discussion,

> a postman, speaking as a member of the church, suggested what might be done: A few could give £5 each; the majority could subscribe £1 each; some might be able only to offer 10s; but the average would be £1 for each man of the congregation, and as there were nine hundred of them, church members, that would mean a sum of £900.[8]

In spite of the financial constraints it was decided there was need for a proper pipe organ to use for the well-attended services. The church agreed to fundraise for £1000 to have a new organ. It was built by William Hill of London. Cuff claimed it was 'the largest and best organ in the North East of London'.[9] There is some weight to his claim, since it still functions today in Holy Trinity Church, Hounslow. The organist in this period was Mr A Tucker, a very able musician. He played for the London Sunday School Choral Society and the annual Protestant Festival at Alexandra Palace. He also gave recitals at the Albert Hall, Crystal Palace and Queen's Hall. The Tabernacle choir he ran was 60 strong and larger for festivals.[10]

As significant as the effort of the members to raise needed funds to sustain the varied work of the church is the contribution of dedicated individuals.

Job E. Wren

One such was Job Wren. He lived in 'social housing' in Peabody Buildings, Spitalfields[11] and came to the church in 1873 when the church was meeting in the Town Hall at the start of Cuff's ministry. He was spiritually awakened by the preaching, was baptised by Cuff and became a member early the following year. He was totally devoted to the church, and to his pastor and father in God. He served and worked, commending himself to the leaders and was appointed as salaried chapel keeper, living rent free in the chapel house in the courtyard of Providence Chapel. When this was torn down for the building of the great Tabernacle, he moved with his wife and family into 20 Hackney Road on the frontage of the new church. The front room was turned into a bookshop which they managed along with other duties.

The spirit in which he served for over 50 years can be seen in his responses to the difficulties over the deteriorating building and stressed finances. He painted windows and did 'many other jobs about the place thereby saving the Church funds many pounds.' He was regularly publicly thanked and given gratuities.[12] Along with his annual amount for a holiday, he received a gift in 1901 for drain work, carpenter's work and for painting the whole of the outside of the School Room.[13]

Ten years later he was still serving in this way when he 'waited upon' the deacons to offer extra work. The deacons 'urged him to take the whole of Friday as a day of rest for himself and Mrs Wren'. She was clearly a devoted worker too. It was agreed to provide money for cover on his day off.[14] The church knew that their Chapel Keeper was a good investment and offered him an extra 7/6 a week. He was happy to accept 5/6.[15] Later his salary rose to £3 a week,[16] but in post-war 1919 his provided uniform was not replaced because of the 'fearful increase in the price of clothes'[17] and a move to reduce his pay was strongly resisted by some, because of his 'long and faithful service'.[18]

He was still painting 'in his own time' in 1922.[19] He was the photographer who took a number of shots of the buildings. However, no photos and no description of his exist. But Job Wren, moving about the church premises in his uniform was a visible and powerful reminder to anyone who came in of the dedication and servant spirit created in working people by the gospel of Christ which William Cuff preached. The church and its work was Wren's discipleship. He did not serve for the financial reward. Other motives were at work rooted in the saving good he found through Shoreditch Baptist Church.

His dedication also survived Cuff's retirement, since he served through the short ministry of Daniel Hayes and beyond. Alfred Butler, who followed, expressed his loving appreciation after eight months at Shoreditch, speaking of 'the very helpful services rendered to himself and the church by the Chapel Keepers Mr and Mrs Wren'.[20] Job Wren died after a short illness in October 1927.

His last recorded special job was to fix the ventilator flues. 'There will be no further troubles as to downdrafts', he said. There were 130 applications for his job.[21]

John Edmonds

As the 20th century advanced the problem of 'small attendance at services' increasingly occupied the deacons.[22] At the May Church Meeting in 1910, 105 members were listed for non-attendance.[23] One solution was to get more help for the pastor, who was now 69 and 'after such a long and arduous ministry' overdue for retirement. The Rev. John Edmonds, originally a Gloucestershire boy like Cuff, had been sent from Shoreditch to the Pastor's College in 1889.[24] He had served as minister at Grimsby and West Green, Tottenham. In June 1913 a very large number of members 'very enthusiastically' called him as co-pastor for a six month trial.

It was an impossible role for an already experienced minister. Nor could the church afford it. He soon asked the deacons for his inadequate £2 a week salary to be reviewed. After 'a very serious discussion' and because it was 'felt that the influence of the work of our Brother Mr Edmonds had not realized our hopes as to increasing the congregations ... or increased financial income,' they could not recommend the church to appoint him permanently. However, they concluded it was wrong to judge results on the basis of the summer months, so they offered him a further twelve months. Half of an agreed £200 salary was now to come from Cuff's income. It was also noted that he had another part-time job and that he was not present every Sunday, as expected. The situation was deteriorating.

By August 1914 the church was £800 overdrawn, with a forecast of worse to come.[25] By October the church was unable to pay either of the pastors. In December Edmonds offered his resignation. There was a strong division of opinion in the church. Some saw that Cuff was now 'unable to carry on the work of this church himself' and wanted Edmonds to remain.[26] After a painful and acrimonious debate, by a majority vote at the church meeting, it was decided he should leave at the end of 1914.[27] The significant tension was diffused by the proposal being handled 'from a financial standpoint'. Edmonds left unhappily and without a formal farewell 'owing to the difference of opinion on the subject'.[28]

Others were now called upon to help, to preach, to lead the midweek services and to assist in pastoral work. The financial situation continued to worsen. Finally in October 1916 Cuff read to the deacons a circular he was sending to all church supporters for his 44th Anniversary hinting at his retirement. The next minute is terse; 'The Brethren seemed so surprised and grieved – that it was received in silence'. At a subsequent meeting they read him their response; 'urging him most earnestly to reconsider … … and to stay with us a till the Homecall comes.' Cuff was 'too much overcome to reply'.[29] The church meeting agreed, but there was no going back. Cuff will retire at the end of 1917. A total of 3,206 members had joined the Tabernacle in his 45 years of ministry. His impact on the area was enormous and in recent years a block of flats has been named after him; Cuff Point in Columbia Road. His final act was to lead communion on Sunday Dec 30th.

The church was soon engaged in the search for a new pastor.

The Shoreditch Tabernacle Cycling Club 1914 with Rev. John Edmonds

Chapter 9

Spirited Sisters

When Cuff finally retired at the end of 1917 the church was without a minister for two years. From the start it was clear that there would be a large gap in leadership as well as serious financial weakness. Money had been regularly made available by the London Baptist Association to meet deficits. In 1916 the Trustees had agreed that the Shoreditch Tabernacle Trust should be transferred from private trustees to the Baptist Union Corporation 'under agreed conditions'.[1] In July the following year terms were proposed by the Baptist Union. They included:

1. A 'finance committee', made up of representatives of the church and the BU, would be formed to supervise the finances for three years.
2. The Tabernacle would be sold and the money used to adapt the Lecture Hall as a chapel. The three houses in Austin Street would be demolished in order to erect School Buildings for at least 500 children.[2]

The deacons all signed up to this plan, but there was consternation among the members. After considerable debate the church agreed to transfer the trust, but refused the plan to demolish the Tabernacle. They also obtained more representation on the Committee.

This arrangement had been successful at Bloomsbury Baptist Church where a joint 'Central Committee' had managed the church since 1906. The London Baptist Association had bought its freehold and, under the influence of the Methodist 'forward movement' and the concept of a 'Central Church', had successfully steered Bloomsbury through its financial and leadership challenges.[3] At Shoreditch the 'Central Church' idea was also present. The members even agreed to rename the church 'Shoreditch Tabernacle Central Church',[4] but they resisted the persuasion of the Baptist Union managers, especially over the proposed demolition of the Tabernacle.

The 'Central' Church name soon disappears. Rumours about the sale of the Tabernacle rolled on for five years, reflecting the members' suspicion of the Central Committee and the control of the LBA. However, the Committee worked well, under the chairmanship of John Ewing, the first Superintended of the Metropolitan Area and secretary of the London Baptist Association. They tried to settle the church finances more securely and began the search for a new pastor.

In July 1918 a meeting of 130 members agreed, with one dissenting, to invite Daniel Hayes of Kensington Tabernacle, Bristol to be pastor for three years, but he declined 'owing to ill-health'. He was 51 and had served as a missionary in the Congo, from where he was invalided home with malaria.[5] After some uncertainty with issues over housing and then a renewed call from the church, Hayes accepted in July 1919.

The terms included Mrs Hayes as a ministry partner, to be paid £50 a year, a most unusual arrangement for the time. The Hayes had trained together for overseas mission at the Regions Beyond Missionary Union centre, Harley College in Bow, and then from 1894 served together in the Congo. On their return Hayes pastored Berger Hall in Poplar, the RBMU connected church with a congregation of one thousand. He and Mrs Hayes worked there together for seventeen years and Hayes, 'preacher, pastor; politician and philanthropist', was elected to the Poplar Borough Council.[6] Mrs Hayes had seen and no doubt ministered with 'the deaconesses with their dark blue uniforms and bonnets' working out of the nearby Doric College, the deaconesses training centre of Harley House.[7] In consequence, the other requirement of the Shoreditch call was that one or two deaconesses would be appointed to assist. The first was 'Sister Laura'. Hayes' insistence on the appointment of these women was a very significant moment in the life of the church.

Daniel Hayes.

The Deaconesses

Deaconesses came to serve the people of Shoreditch in a long and influential succession for the next 50 years. 'Sister Laura' had been working at Vernon King's Cross Baptist Church and she started work in October 1919 in Shoreditch. Then Sister Ivy came in April 1921.[8] These were not 'women deacons' as we might say today. Most churches then were not ready to accept women as 'leaders' of the church. They were appointed as pastoral and missional assistants to the minister under the authority of the elders and deacons. We might call them Community Workers now. This was not a new idea to Shoreditch. In fact, the next door Mildmay Hospital had its own band of deaconesses, created and trained in 1860 by the founders William and Catherine Pennefather, to work in the poverty and ill-health of the area. Some had been sent to the locality of the church during the cholera epidemic of 1866.⁹

The London Baptist Association 'Forward Movement' formed a Deaconesses Order in 1891 and very quickly offered William Cuff a deaconess to work with him in the Tabernacle. The deacons decided they could not afford it.¹⁰ Then in 1906, aware of excellent work done by deaconesses in other areas and seeing the impossible weight of pastoral responsibility on Cuff and his elders in a church of almost 1000 members, the church, after some debate, appointed twelve 'Deaconesses'. These were essentially the deacons' wives plus Mrs Cuff. It was not a great shift of policy, since most of them had been doing this work anyway: pastoral visiting, running children's and women's meetings and caring for the bereft and sick in the community.

However, what Mr and Mrs Hayes asked for when they arrived was different. Their plan kick-started a 50 year sequence of over 25 deaconesses who served at the Tabernacle, together with its mission at Queen's Road and, after its wartime destruction, at Pownall Road.

> They wore a distinctive form of dress which at first served not merely as a mark of office but also as a protection in days when it was unwise for a woman to be about the streets of London alone once darkness had fallen... ... a tailored navy-blue coat, or coat and skirt, worn with a close fitting navy-blue bonnet from which hung a grey veil.¹¹

S. Laura, first Shoreditch deaconess.

The story of Shoreditch Tabernacle would not have been the same without them. In their highly visible uniforms, they worked in social and pastoral care of members and others, ministered among women and young people, taking full responsibility for whole sections of church life. Home visiting was their primary task.

Most of the Shoreditch deaconesses were formally trained at a deaconesses college, or similar institution; some were educated to degree level. From 1919 the Baptist Union took responsibility for their supervision. Many of them chose, when it was offered in 1975, to become accredited Baptist Ministers. The deaconesses took the title 'Sister', although for some serving in Shoreditch it seems to have been a locally attributed term of respect. They also were in the habit of taking new, professional first names, which is confusing in the records. When some subsequently married and changed their second name as well their trail is even more difficult to follow. In the following narrative, where available, full names are given with the dates of their time at Shoreditch.

IT IS WORTH WHILE
Supporting the Work of the Tabernacle!

OUR ACTIVITIES:

CHILDREN'S CHURCH	BROTHERHOOD
YOUNG WORSHIPPERS' LEAGUE	MEN'S INSTITUTE
SUNDAY SCHOOLS	LADS' INSTITUTE
BIBLE CLASSES	GIRLS' INSTITUTE
BAND OF HOPE	GYMNASIUM
JUNIOR C.E.	SICK CLUB (700 members)
BABIES' CRECHE	WOMEN'S MEETING
CHURCH	RESCUE WORK
	OPEN AIR WORK
GIRLS' LIFE BRIGADE	FRESH AIR FUND
BOYS' LIFE BRIGADE	HOLIDAY CLUBS
CHILDREN'S PLAY HOUR	CLOTHING CLUBS
GIRLS' SOCIAL HOUR	RELIEF WORK
YOUNG PEOPLE'S FELLOWSHIP	

HOXTON HOUSE MISSION
QUEEN'S ROAD MISSION

An Institutional Church, 1919

The church and work which Mr and Mrs Hayes and the two deaconesses inherited in 1919 was very demanding. There were 645 members and complex associated missions and 'institutions'. They included a cycling club. The return of soldiers from the Great War added new pastoral and missional challenges. A service and tea organized to welcome home 'our boys' was attended by 200 men in May 1919. A year later William Cuff unveiled a memorial to men from the church lost in the conflict. It names thirteen who died, including the Cuff's son-in-law Frederick Leslie 'Cuff' Link, killed in 1919 in an air accident, and a further six who survived the war. Research by Susan Tredinnik, held at the church, details the records of each of these men:

William Clarke, Percy Dickins, John (Tom) Fisher, George Fountain, Walter Gartan, Stanley Groome, Humphrey Hayes, William Hicks, Frederick 'Cuff' Link, Richard Parsons, Frederick Rogers, William Stanton, and Edwin Williams.

Those who survived were Harry Bristow, William (Charles) Dexter, Albert Durant, Albert Rouse, Samuel Solomon and Ernest Percival Thompson.[12]

To meet the need of the returning soldiers a Young Men's Institute was proposed. But the culture was changing fast and tensions are illustrated by debates in this period over the Institute. In a time of increasing economic depression the church offered opportunity for friendship support, social contact and self-made entertainment as well as for mission. Many men returned from the war with a smoking habit. The leaders of the Young Men's Institute wanted to allow smoking in their allocated rooms and they also wanted to play billiards. Messrs. Goodman and Dean presented these proposals to the Church Meeting. Some in the church resisted it, seeing only 'worldliness'. The billiards issue was postponed for three months until the new pastor arrived, but smoking was to be allowed 'in the young men's rooms'. The mission opportunity was perceived and held open by most of the members, even though the deacons were 'unanimously against smoking and billiards'.[13]

One of Daniel Hayes' first tasks on appointment was to examine and revise the membership roll. Many were removed so that in 1921 300 members are recorded. Evans astutely points out that this is 'only 50 more than the 1870 figure' when Cuff began his ministry.[14] By July that year the finances were again in trouble and the Committee were unable to help with the expected £600 deficit. Hayes was 'cast down and giving up the struggle'. The following year was the height of the post-war depression and with no further help possible from the BU or the LBA the deacons met a deficit by personal loans.[15] It is no surprise to find that in spite of strong appeals by both deacons and members to remain, Hayes resigned in March 1922. 'One of the most lovable men in the ministry, with a big heart and a passion for souls' he had served admirably and wisely for three years, commending himself to the people in a very difficult period. They were sad to see him leave for a new ministry in

A. H. Tyler
Church Secretary 1922-1941

Clacton-on-Sea and his memory 'would leave much fragrance behind it'.[16]

Again the church had to find a new pastor. People rallied round to help. Five new deacons were appointed raising their number to 12, Cuff came back to preach sometimes, to organise the anniversary services and to raise funds so that over the next few months he managed to cover the deficit of £750. Dr. John Ewing conducted baptisms. Sister Laura was to be present at Deacons' Meetings, although 'attempting to do too much now' she became 'seriously ill' and Mrs Cuff was invited to help cover her duties. She finally resigned in May 1923 through 'continual ill-health' and died in October.[17] A. H. Tyler became Church Secretary and served for the next nineteen years.

Quite swiftly the church settled on Alfred Butler, pastor of Mitcham Lane, Streatham. In February 1923 he accepted a strong call from the church (although to his irritation the *British Weekly* had already announced it). William Cuff's shadow still lay long over the church; 'my methods may differ from those of my esteemed predecessor' Butler said, but he felt there was 'a great work to be done at the Tabernacle'.[18]

The LBA had promised support of £30 a year,[19] and he began ministry on Sunday May 6th. The deacons were united in support, placing on record,

Alfred Butler

> our esteem for our pastor Rev Alfred Butler – our deep conviction from his life and labour amongst us – that he is the sent of God to this church, the friend and brother to us all – and we are looking forward to a long and a very helpful pastorate full of blessing, and bringing great glory to God. We on our part are determined to support him in every way, and help to bring about all we desire for the church and the Kingdom of our God.[20]

The church was again in good heart: more hymnbooks for increasing congregations were bought. A new deaconess Sister Margaret (May Lofts, 1923-27) was 'happy with growing work among the women'. The following year a further deaconess, Sister Ruth (Ruth Dyer, 1924-25), joined the staff free of cost to the church. In 1923 the church formed a Girls' Life Brigade, 'an organisation which was to have a great influence on many young people throughout the following years, as was shown by the 1984 reunion' and a Boys' Brigade company, the 117th London Company, a year later.[21] By February 1924, 69 new members had been added and 59 had been baptised by Butler. The church trust still stated a 'closed membership' position, a clear incentive for converts to be baptised.[22]

The church reported in April to the Joint Committee about,

> the great success of our Pastor Rev Alfred Butler – in every way - larger congregations, financial success - finer spirit - and above all great spiritual gains - the church being built up and many new members joining, nearly 100 since our pastor came. We thank God and take courage.[23]

A church and congregation Social Hour in February 1925 with 'very many young people present' heard 'most gratifying reports' from 24 'missions'; activities and meetings run by the church. As well as a general report by the secretary on the life of the Church, these were:

Sunday School
Women's Meeting
Crèche
Hoxton House Mission School
Shap Street Mission School
Young People Society
Bible Class Young Women
Bible Class Young Men
Mission Service
Open Air service
Gymnasium
Primary Department (afternoon)
Primary Department (evening)
Sick Benefits Society
Girls' Life Brigade
Boys' Life Brigade
Missionary Work
Girls Social
Young Men's Training Class
Band of Hope
Choir
Internation[al] Bible Reading Association
Young People's Prayer Meeting
Christmas Gift Fund [24]

Alfred Butler and his leaders were heading up a complex and demanding church, which was now beginning to grow after a time of decline. However, the threat of inadequate income was still present. The church auditor 'gave his opinion that the financial need of the church made our pastor's work very hard indeed'.[25] A controversial scheme of numbered offering envelopes was introduced; only if individuals wanted to use them.[26] But still an £800 deficit was expected for 1925.

Other challenges occupied the leaders from time to time, most related to the social conditions surrounding the church. Some members were strict teetotallers and in the area around the church drink was a major problem. The deacons had a 'long and wearying discussion' on the proposal that 'deacons elected should be total abstainers'. This was not accepted.[27]

The Austin Street houses (Nos. 33, 35 and 37) were falling into ruin and eating up money for repairs, while the rents were continually in arrears. Number 33 was finally condemned in 1933.[28] The health of the pastor and deaconesses was a reoccurring concern. Overwork, as well as close contact with poor and unhealthy people, left them vulnerable. One Deaconess applied and was declared 'not suitable as she declined slum work'.[29] Sister Margaret Lofts eventually 'resigned though ill-health'.[30] In April 1926 Butler was 'absent through serious nervous breakdown' and was advised to take a long rest. He remained off work until October, when he tried to return for Sundays only. In the following January the deacons extended his leave, since 'it would never do to have another breakdown.'[31]

The deaconesses stood in, on one Sunday Sister Margaret 'serving so well in taking two services'. Both deaconesses preached on Thursdays. Women were being allowed to make their mark in public ministry. Butler never fully returned to work. At the end of 1927 after only four years at Shoreditch he accepted a call to New Southgate.[32]

Significant events in 1927 mark the end of an era for the church. Job Wren, the endlessly serving chapel keeper, died on October 14th. George Cartwright, the local grocer, baptized by Cuff in 1874 died in his sleep on July 1st. He had been the mainstay of the administration of the church for over 50 years; godly and trusted as Cuff's 'armour bearer' he continued to serve the subsequent ministers with equal loyalty. He is named in a plaque in the Tab Centre. Marianne Maria Cuff died in 1924 and the still greatly venerated William Cuff on 31st May, 1926 at the age of 86. For his last days he was back in Gloucestershire and died in his native village of Hasfield. He was buried with honour in Abney Park Cemetery, Hoxton, beside Marianne and the small son, William, they had lost. You can visit his memorial there to this day.

The carefully kept record of attendance at communion, with a tick each month against each member's name, shows for William Cuff a full line of ticks month after month. Then his absence from his beloved people and Tabernacle is finally registered with a long line of blanks.

Marianne and William Cuff in later life

Chapter 10

Repair and Recovery

The London Baptist Association and the Baptist Union argued for the disposal of the Tabernacle building. The deacon disagreed strongly. They were seeking recovery and advance with a new pastor.[1] On 18th November 1928 Earnest Oscar Clifford, MA HCF (Honorary Chaplain to the Forces) preached with a view to the pastorate. He was the son of a Sunderland shipwright and an amateur player for Sunderland Football club. He had graduated from St Catherine's College, Oxford and trained for Baptist ministry at Regent's Park College.

As a services chaplain during the war he had suffered from shell shock. The only lasting effect of this was weakness in his right hand which meant he always typed, except when he signed his name.[2] He had worked for nine years very happily with his brother, Paul Rowntree Clifford, at West Ham Central Mission where his first wife, Laura, died. Here he met and married Ruth Holmes one of the Mission's deaconesses.[3] At West Ham he ran seven football teams as an arm of evangelistic outreach and played in the first team, as a result seeing a number of men come to faith and to the church.[4] He had not thought of leaving and at first refused the Shoreditch invitation, overawed by the enormous needs of the district. The deacons in turn were not sure; his 'voice seemed the drawback'. But by January they were united in their

Ruth Clifford

Earnest Clifford

recommendation and the church meeting agreed to invite him for a first period of three years, although a substantial group voted to the contrary.

The Central Committee confirmed the decision and raised the offer of salary by £100 to £450 a year.[5] As he reconsidered the call, Clifford felt he had heard a voice saying 'Behold I have set before thee an open door; go forward nothing doubting, for I have sent thee'.[6] He began in May 1929.

The Tabernacle itself was hardly an encouraging sight. It was dirty and neglected, badly in need of repairs because of rotten window frames and crumbling stonework. It was 'a huge Victorian shell of a place, built with the aim of covering the largest area possible at the least expense'.[7] Two years later an insecure iron front gate fell on a boy who subsequently died. The church paid funeral costs, but avoided liability. Insurances were revised upwards.[8]

9-23, Austin Street in 1944

The three houses in Austin Street were in disrepair. There was no house for the Cliffords until the following December, when they moved into Queen Elizabeth's Walk, Stoke Newington. He was immediately presented with challenging pastoral and relationship issues. Job Wren's grandson, who had been given his honoured grandfather's post as Chapel Keeper, was disciplined with regard to his work and about a personal relationship. After interviews with the new pastor and no change of behaviour his employment was terminated.[9] In the Boys'

Brigade there was 'serious trouble among the acting officers' and no Captain.[10]

The membership had declined by about two thirds over the previous 20 years, being 260 in October 1929. But in many other ways the church was thriving, in spite of eighteen months without a pastor and recently declining membership. There was an elected body of twelve loyal deacons and a number of honoured life deacons. The church still had great influence in the community. One deacon, Richard E. Pearson, was a Justice of the Peace, a Bethnal Green councillor and Mayor in 1931.

The twenty or more church organisations and meetings were in reasonably good heart. Reports to the members in March 1929 show 70 in the Young People's Association; the Women's Meetings with 279 on the register and the Girls' Life Brigade with 91 members. The local missions and Sunday Schools, supported by the Tabernacle and partly staffed by many members and older teenagers of the mother church, continued strongly. At Shap Street Mission in 1929 the Sunday School alone had an average attendance of 304 in their three sessions and ran other meetings and evangelistic efforts. There were no deficits in 1929 and 1930.[11] This is not a failing church by any means.

The Tabernacle Sunday School in the 1930s.

The arrival of Clifford and his wife Ruth, herself a trained deaconess and an able public speaker and writer, gave new impetus to everything. Clifford was a thoughtful manager and an interesting and persuasive preacher. He also worked very hard. Members 'recall him working from ten in the morning until ten at night at the Tabernacle' as well as engaging in pastoral visiting.[12] Substantial and urgently needed restoration work on the Tabernacle was completed in 1931 at an eventual cost of £7,500. During the work, services were held in the Lecture Hall, the Mildmay Mission Hall and the London Music Hall in the High Street.[13] This large debt lingered for nearly fifteen years. Wide appeal was made for finance and funds were also raised by events, such as the Christmas Fair over three days in 1933, with entertainment and stalls manned by church departments. The Boys' Brigade and Life Boys ran the Parcel Stand. They declared,

> Here you may leave whatever you do not wish to carry about. (Babies not accepted). You will then be able to promenade easily, to take refreshments, and your hands will be free to reach your pockets.

When the restoration was finished Clifford wrote,

> Five years ago Shoreditch Tabernacle was in danger of being closed. The magnificent buildings reflected some of the glory of former prosperous days, but they had become dilapidated. There were widening cracks in the main walls. The ceiling had fallen in several places. Gallery stairways were condemned. The sanitary conditions could not be worse.[14]

Somehow the church was at the same time able to continue to support two or, at times, three paid Deaconesses to assist, although they were not paid much, considering their work a sacrificial calling.[15] They were usually appointed with the help of Miss Doris M. Rose, the respected administrator of the Order of Baptist Deaconesses, which had been adopted by the Baptist Union in 1919.

The influence of these trained women and their contribution to the Shoreditch church, well before and during the time of Clifford's ministry, is enormous. At this time they were formally invited to attend deacons' meetings and so engaged in the management of the church.[16] By 1936 the Women's Meeting membership

Sister Pauline

was nine hundred, made up of a Monday afternoon meeting led by Ruth Clifford, a Tuesday evening meeting led by Sister Pauline (Alice Clara Morris, 1935-38) and a young wives' meeting on Thursdays.

When they went on an outing they needed nine coaches. There were meetings at the Tabernacle every night for young people. Sister Pauline wrote in 1937 that 'Rooms and Halls are occupied every evening of the week by groups, companies, and fellowships of young people: Boys' and Girls' Brigades, Junior, Intermediate and Senior Christian Endeavour, Missionary Circle, Girls and Lad's Clubs, Gymnasium.' For these the Tabernacle was a 'home from home, a place of comfort and congenial friendship, where a large majority of our young people live from the time they leave work until bedtime.'[17]

Sister Dorothy (Dorothy Finch, 1938-46) wrote that her 'first recollection of Shoreditch Tabernacle was the young people's fellowship held in the Lecture Hall. Over 100 young people were singing, as only Shoreditch folk can sing'.[18] They increasingly were called on to preach at mid-week services and to lead worship on Sundays. They strengthened the later acceptance of deaconesses as accredited Baptist ministers.[19] Sister Hilda (Hilda Bromley, 1938-39) and Sister Dorothy were the first to be welcomed to deacons' meetings.

Sister Jesse

Sister Hilda

A measure of the affection in which they were held, which also spelled difficulties, is seen in Sister Marjorie (Marjorie Owen, 1935-37). Her work as 'visiting sister' at Queen's Road had to end because of lack of finances. The deacons were troubled by the fact that she 'had influenced some of the young people to leave with her'.[20] Their ultimate motivation was clear. Sister Jessie (Katherine Tebbutt, 1934-38) writes about the children of the church, 'we aim to set before our children the highest aim of all, that of being followers of Jesus Christ, and many have been those who have responded to that challenge.'[21]

As the agreed three years of Clifford's contract came to an end the deacons unanimously recommended he be asked to remain 'without any time limit'. The church agreed enthusiastically, even though the London Baptist Association would now withdraw their £100 of support for his stipend.[22] The management of the church was set up with Clifford, the treasurer G.B. Cartwright (the son of George Cartwright) and the Secretary A. H. Tyler forming what we would call a leadership team, supported by up to fourteen deacons. In 1933 these were Messrs. Baynton, Bocking, Bradbridge, Corrigan, Duncombe, Garrod, Hudson, Husbands, Mills, Owen, Shorey, Stean, Wyman and Councillor Richard Pearson, JP. Women were represented by Mrs Clifford and deaconesses, Sister Mary (Mary Smith, 1930) and Sister Bertha (Bertha Beale, 1930-35).[23] The church organised, or sponsored seventeen departments and ministries, including a 'sick club' with 700 members and a thriving Sunday School.

Sister Bertha

A major shift in the effort of the church in this period was with regard to the neighbouring church at Queen's (now Queensbridge) Road. For a number of years they had been appealing for help in both personnel and finance. The deacons resisted these approaches.[24] In 1932 however the long-standing mission and Sunday School in Shap Street moved into the Queen's Road premises.[25] This changed the attitude to Queen's Road church and Shoreditch took it over on 1st January 1933. The remaining members were now to be members of Shoreditch Tabernacle; an increase of 50 members is reflected in annual returns.[26] Later, one of the three Deaconesses was stationed there. The Hoxton House Mission was also still being supported from the Tabernacle.

It was a separate and different church, however, and the move contained inherent problems. A confrontation over the united women's meeting annual excursion to the seaside illustrates the challenge. One Tuesday evening the deacons received a deputation from the leaders of the Queen's Road women. It had been noted that 'certain of the women from Queen's Road women's meeting had gone from the charabancs into the public houses and their leaders had permitted this'. The pastor made it clear this was not to be allowed. The minute records that the women's deputation 'were inclined to resent our attitude' and would merely consider the matter.[27] To respond to the missional opportunity, a deacon's daughter, Sister Marjorie (Owen) was invited to work at Queen's Road.[28] But the new venture needed continual funding, so the Tabernacle gave annual grants between £40 and £90 to sustain it.

... from the charabancs ...

The 1930s was the time of the Great Depression and many strangers came to the area; some to seek work others to hide their poverty in a desperately poor area. After the payment of staff stipends the next largest item listed every year is 'Relief distribution, Appeals, Holidays, Xmas, etc.' In 1941 this item exceeded the pastor's stipend. The church was still looking after the Shoreditch poor in very large measure.

The 1930s Survey of London found over 10% of the local population living more than three to a room. Birth rates and death rates, as well as infant mortality, were still high. Grocery and coal tickets, baskets of food and clothing were constantly being given away to people in great need. This work was redoubled at Christmas, when parcels were distributed, with toys for the children and the famous dinners initiated by Cuff continued.

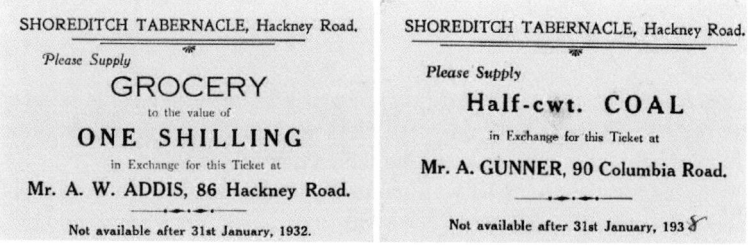

Clifford's approach to Christian mission was clear; the gospel of Jesus is central but the care of the poor is essential. In 1937 he wrote,

> We are living in a day when the great danger is to lose sight of the individual in the mass – the labourer in the Labour

movement – the welfare of the individual in the welfare of the City – the relief of the poor family in the problem of poverty – the sick and suffering in the problem of disease. It is praiseworthy that the political and social parties should seek the welfare of the masses, but we must not forget that character is at the root of all social problems.[29]

He saw the church as a centre of practical care and a 'Witness for Jesus Christ in one of London's Darkest Districts'. There is substance to this claim. This was a church touching thousands of lives for good with 'the 900 mothers attending the Sisterhoods – the 1,000 children associated with the Sunday Schools and Children's Church – the Brotherhood – the Sick Benefit Society – the Young People's Organisations – the Relief and Rescue work – the Fresh Air Fund'.

Annual outings to the seaside or country were part of the church programme and the 'Holiday Homes' scheme was revived, through a relative of Mrs Clifford who owned *The Daily Sketch*. The newspaper began to sponsor holidays for people in need so local women 'who had never known the joy of a single holiday' were able to get away to recover their health. One said, 'This is the second holiday I have had in twenty-seven years of married life.' Many children got their first glimpse of the sea on a *Daily Sketch* holiday. 'My wife' wrote one husband, 'has never had a holiday before and she will have cause to bless you for a very long time. She and the baby have returned looking the picture of health'.[30]

It was the Deaconesses who made the connections to the women in need. Sister Pauline writes of one visit,

> Mrs D… was busy washing. Her husband, unemployed, was tidying the room which was a kitchen, living room and bedroom in one. She attended the Women's Meeting and the services in the Tabernacle. Last year, through the kindness of friends who give to the holiday fund, she spent a fortnight in

the country. How enthusiastically she spoke of that unforgettable rest and change; 'That was the first time I saw the country and it made me think.' It had been the first step to lead her to the saviour.[31]

Membership numbers and congregations were sustained by newcomers.

> Beattie Ellett remembers nervously walking up and down outside in order to pluck up enough courage to go in. When she did, she was astonished at the warmth of the handshake of the Deacons at the door and the welcome from Mrs. Clifford. Once inside, she listened entranced to Sister Pauline singing by the organ. Beattie thought that in her grey veil she looked very like Nurse Cavell. Beattie was baptised in 1936.[32]

Violet Julier was a small girl attending the Old Nichol Street mission, led by the able and dedicated Richard Pearson. In 1938, when she was just seven, the mission finally closed and she went with many others to Shoreditch Tabernacle. Vi sometimes played the organ for worship and recalls congregations of 200 and memorable services. Mr Tucker the organist let her go into the Tabernacle to practise. In 1944 Clifford baptised her mother, using a chair because of illness and her father was baptised three years later. The Sunday School had 150 children and five departments. Vi first taught in the Beginners with seven other teachers who, she says, 'were fabulous'.[33]

During all these years the Restoration Debt had burdened the church. Money had been raised by Clifford's appeals to friends and churches throughout the country. The annual 'Sale of Work', a regular feature of the church for many years, and gift days at the time of the Pastor's anniversary, kept finances afloat. As the debt began to diminish two deacons, George B. Cartwright and Richard Pearson, each gave £500. With a last great effort the Restoration Deficit was finally cleared in 1944.[34]

Work was done 'in a spirit of good fellowship' in 1939 to redecorate the Lecture Hall. It consisted of an eight-week effort by the teachers and scholars to raise 1000 shillings to redecorate their large school by voluntary labour. The Girls' Life Brigade and the lady teachers did all the cleaning and washing down paint, while the Boys' Brigade, male teachers, members of the Men's Club and other friends did the re-decorating.[35]

But German bombers soon undid all the efforts to maintain the buildings.

Chapter 11

Bombed and Blessed

Incendiary bombs fell on the church buildings on Sunday evening, December 29th 1940, during an intense air raid on the City of London. When the siren went at 6.05 p.m. the after-church 'Song Service' was taking place in the Ladies Hall next to the School Hall. 100,00 fire bombs were dropped that night and two fell on the roof of the School, fire falling down to burn out the centre of the wooden floor. One caught in the roof trusses and threatened to destroy the whole building. The young men from the next door meeting immediately went into action. Harrison records the event.

> [T]he thin walls, beginning to bow outward, were bound together by steel rods which crossed the building. There were no pillars supporting the roof, just an immense expanse of ceiling extending high over a vast empty space. One night ... an incendiary bomb fell through the roof and onto these high rafters, threatening to set fire to the building. While the raid was still in progress, Bob Batt, then a deacon of the church, and others, risked their lives in climbing across the joists to reach the bomb and put it out.[1]

They also found another incendiary that had fallen on the Tabernacle and fallen right through the roof. 'Several young fellows' tackled that one too. Outside, fire engines were rushing to the firestorm in the City, but someone managed to stop one.

'This is a shelter for people,' he shouted, 'you've got to stop!'[2]

The fire officers put a final end to the fire danger. But the centre of the School roof was destroyed and the floor was considerably damaged. The Tabernacle damage was slight and soon repaired by Government funding. The young men were not the only ones in action. The deaconess, Sister Alice (Alice Redfern, 1940-42), was also present and took a leading role in the firefighting. She was later commended by the church for 'the courage shown' on that fearful night.[3]

The mission church at Queen's Road and the Pownall Road School buildings were also hit that evening by incendiaries and blast from High Explosive bombs. They were 'quite unusable' and Queen's Road church never reopened for services.[4] Because the Shoreditch School Hall was a 'third line rest centre', the roof was quickly repaired by the Government. A team of fire watchers were belatedly organized and blackout for the church was put in place. Vi Julier recalls that they slept at night in the Deaconesses Room (on the right of the tabernacle stage) the Deacons Room, (on its left) and in the Pastor's Office (in the middle).[5]

The war disrupted or changed much church activity. The 6.30 evening services were moved to Sunday afternoon, although they moved back each year when light evenings came. A number of organisations were suspended, including the Boys' Brigade. The officers and deacons were to be retained in position 'for the duration of the war'. The church became a place of refuge for those bombed out of their houses. The Queen's Road Girls' Life Brigade was combined with the Tabernacle company.[6]

Violet Julier

Equally difficult was the movement of people away from the area. When the war broke out in 1939 most children and some of the mothers of the area were sent to the country. They soon returned, but were evacuated again when the bombing of London began in earnest on 7th September 1940. All the children from the mission at Hoxton House went away and the mission closed, never to reopen. The Clifford's son David was evacuated with his school in 1943 to Cumberland.[7] There were 57 young men of the church away on active service.[8] One record indicates that 72 members were called away for military service, many never to return. [9]A deacon, Bob Batt, records that about 50 past and present members of the Boys' Brigade were serving in the forces and noted that the captain, his fellow deacon 'Skipper Stean, burns gallons of midnight oil and wears out innumerable pens in a valiant endeavour to keep in touch with them all.'[10]

Significant young leaders were also lost. Clifford had just found a very able ally in his newly appointed church secretary, F. M. W. (Fred) Harrison. Trained as a pharmacist at Manchester University he now worked in London for Boots the Chemist. The Cliffords looked after the young single man and he and Clifford became friends, regularly lunching together on Sundays. Harrison was in a reserved occupation and so exempt from military call-up. But he resigned from his church roles in September 1940 when he was sent by Boots to manage their wholesale department in Calcutta. The army claimed him after Pearl Harbour and he subsequently became a 2nd Lieutenant in the Indian Army, then a Captain and a Major, although in an administrative role.[11] Of this decision he records:

> At this juncture it became necessary for me to register for the army. I had given serious thought to this. The very idea of warfare was abhorrent, yet the decision was not simple. It seemed that Hitler was such an evil man that I should register without claiming to be a pacifist. Accordingly I did so.[12]

Clifford was deeply affected by his departure. Writing later he says, 'I shall never forget my feelings when you told me of your appointment to India… I could think of no one to take your place.' In a later recollection he writes, 'Often I wish that you were here with us.'[13]

And Harrison was not the only one. Clifford faced up to the 'poverty of leadership' in London Churches. His able and loyal leader, G. B. Cartwright, was away most of the time in High Wycombe, as was Richard Pearson. The Pearsons lost their house and all furniture in one raid.[14] The reliable, A. H. Tyler, who had been a faithful member since 1880, a deacon for 25 years and the church secretary for eighteen years, died in March 1940.[15] Clifford says of his church secretary, who succeeded and served right through the war years, 'If it were not for Mr Symons who spends all his leisure at the church I am afraid that it would be impossible to continue.'[16]

G. B. Cartwright

There were the constant pastoral issues of course. Most distressing was 'matter of some delicacy' in 1941. An unnamed young lady, 'formerly a member and good worker for many years had caused disturbance in the services on two occasions'. Her grievance was against one of the deacons, Mr A. Baynton. He was urged by the deacons 'to make a settlement' and was not to attend church until he had done so. He did not comply and on Clifford's advice resigned as a deacon and from church membership. Mrs Baynton, (who had been Sister Jessie[17]) leader of the Women's Meeting formerly at Queen's Road, also resigned.[18] Clifford found this sort of issue very hard to bear. No details are given, but Clifford declared, 'His past has been revealed and it was impossible for him to continue'.[19]

The work did not stop, however. The Cliffords laboured endlessly to sustain three services on Sundays (morning, evening and the 6.30 Song Service) and the ongoing pastoral care, as well as other weekday meetings. There was an eager and thankful spirit in the church in spite of the severe disruption. The church took on an extra two deaconesses, bringing the total to four for a short time in 1942. These are named as Sisters Dorothy Finch (1938-46), Alice Redfern (1940-42), Violet (1941-43) and Bertha. But Alice Redfern died in April 1942 and Sister Violet was ill and transferred to Luton in June 1943. Sister Bertha Beal had served before and was temporary, but the church could not afford to continue her support. The solution to these losses was that Ruth Clifford took up deaconess duties for a modest stipend of £60 a year. Sister Marjorie (Marjorie Lilian Howden, 1944-50) was appointed in October 1944[20] and later Sister Mary (Mary Williams, 1946-49).

Sister Violet

Sister Mary

During the war creative strategies emerged, both for fellowship and witness. Beattie Ellett, who led the Young Worshipper's League at this time, had vivid memories of the Blitz. David Evans wrote up her recollections.

Clifford was often unable to get home at night during the air raids, and so had a bed made up in the organ loft. Mrs. Clifford sometimes joined him. One Sunday night after the evening service, he spotted Agnes Salmon and Beattie Ellett going to shelter in the Old Street Tube Station, suitcases in hand.
"Where are you two going?" he asked.
"Old Street Tube," they replied.
"Well, go tonight, but don't go any more. I'll see you tomorrow,"

Sister Dorothy

Sister Alice

Clifford went out and bought some low beds and Agnes and Beattie slept in the boiler room in the cellars of the Tabernacle for two and a half years. Others joined them, until there were about a dozen staying there as the bombs fell all around. On Saturday nights Agnes would cook egg, bacon and chips on a small primus stove - then a bomb would fall, the lights would go out and they would have to grope around for candles. Whenever anything fell nearby they used to go out and see if they could help, but when incendiaries hit Howard Walls factory opposite the Tabernacle the fire was so great that they could not get out of the Tabernacle until midday, and the front of the building was scorched.[21]

Sister Dorothy later wrote,

> How well we remember one Sunday evening. Outside blackness – guns booming, bombs falling. Inside about 60 met for a Song Service. We talked together before leaving.
> 'Our parents and neighbours are in the shelters - if only they could share our singing, how different they would feel'.

> So the idea took form and we organised three parties to take services in three shelters each Sunday evening and concerts each Wednesday.[22]

With Bill Simmonds and his family they loaded a small piano on a barrow, put on their Brodie tin helmets and went out to the shelters and other refuges to sing and give out literature.

Clifford and his people refused to 'take up a defeatist attitude' and there was much to encourage. The membership was still over 300. In addition to Sunday services, sixteen spiritual, social and worship organisations are listed in March 1942. The minute states 'the number of lives being reached is amazing and our opportunities are great'. Clifford wrote to Harrison on 8th April, 1942.

> All goes well at Shoreditch. The congregations are good considering the number who have been evacuated. The Sunday School adds to its numbers weekly. We have re-commenced the Boys' Brigade. Mixed Clubs for ages 12 to 16 and over 16 have been formed. The Boys' Reserves under the Leadership of Sister Violet number over 30.

Much of the work among young people was sustained. A Young People's meeting, led by Miss Godier, had 'a splendid atmosphere' and the Christian Endeavour group, led by Sister Dorothy, was thriving. The School Hall was crowded for their anniversary, addressed by the Rev. Geoffrey King of East London Tabernacle. A Young People's Day on 21 June began with a 7 a.m. service which seventy attended. They were then served breakfast and by 9 a.m. the hall was full for the Conference. A certain Dr Young led the evening service.[23]

One incident reflects the resilience of Londoners and the place of the Tabernacle in people's lives. Clifford records that one night,

> as I sat in my vestry I had an unexpected visitor. He was one who had lost his house and all his possessions in a raid. He and his wife and others had spent three weeks in our Hall – a Rest Centre. "My insurance policy has matured" he said "and I have been wondering what would be a good investment. I have decided that the best investment is Shoreditch Tabernacle' and he presented me with a gift for £500!

Eighteen month later there was still activity and encouragement, especially among the youth and children's workers, as the Christian Endeavour group report for 1943 shows.

> The work of the Tabernacle is still going on, although many of our active members have been called up during this last year, and of course, this has caused a serious depletion of teachers etc., which is very difficult to make up; however it has not cut down any of the activities, and in fact, an extra meeting has recently been commenced for children on Saturday afternoon called Sunshine Corner, where talking films ranging from the ever popular POPEYE, to the more educational type of travel and religious stories, are shown to a very appreciative audience of over 200 children. Our Church Secretary, Mr Symons, who seems to have a never failing source of energy and time for anything connected with the 'Tab', takes this meeting assisted by Sister Dorothy ... As has been the practice for the last four years, it is planned to give a Christmas Dinner to 200 Old Age Pensioners in the Lecture Hall on Christmas Day; since the first week of December there have been meetings and consultations as to how this tremendous task will be achieved, and as in previous years, it is hoped to obtain eight or nine turkeys for the Dinner, through the medium of various members.[24]

Christmas Dinner for 200 in the Lecture Hall, 1942

The church continued to serve many people unable, or unwilling to move away from wartime danger. The church was for them 'a symbol of the love of God and as such is beloved of them, and even in times of danger they have been reluctant to go away from it.' Arrangements were made for one woman 'to go to a safer area, but she refused to go. When asked why, she replied: "If they could put the Tabernacle on wheels so that I could take it with me I would go." The Tabernacle was the outward expression of her love for the Saviour.'

Shoreditch Baptist Church has never courted controversy. However, in the middle of the war, in the summer of 1942, the church created a minor storm in the Baptist world. On Whit Sunday evening, 24th May, Clifford 'preached a wonderful sermon on baptism' and then baptized seven people in the Tabernacle. At the end of the service he made an appeal, saying 'if any friend was not clear about our beliefs he would be pleased to speak to them' and invited anyone wanting to be baptized in response to the witness and the preaching to give their names to one of the Sisters before leaving the church. In a letter to Fred Harrison he records what happened next.

> As I came out of the Baptistry I announced a hymn. During the singing of the hymn a lady walked down the aisle to be followed by Dr Young who is a house surgeon at Mildmay - a Cambridge blue and Rugger International. Two more men and a lady came forward. All expressed a wish to be baptised there and then.

Sister Dorothy and Symons, the Church Secretary, spoke with them and assured the pastor that immediate baptism would be appropriate. Then they found baptism gowns for them. Clifford explains,

> I ascended the pulpit and said that the Service would continue. We sang a hymn and at the close I baptised the Five. ... ... it was such a unique experience. I have never known it to happen in any Church in England. I am told that it has taken place on the Mission Field. It was a real Pentecostal experience. When I enter[ed] the Church from my Vestry there were excited groups everywhere.[25]

The *Baptist Times* picked up the story and was encouraging, but noted that 'all were strangers to the Tabernacle' and although this had never happened in the church before it was 'a fine tribute to the value and power of our ordinance'.[26]

Not everyone was so enthusiastic, however, and a debate ensued in the Baptist Union about the relationship between conversion, baptism and church membership. Some took the view that formal visitation of the candidates, then discipleship and preparation classes leading to baptism and membership, was the right way. Others said that immediate baptism was fine in some circumstances, since baptism is 'the climax of conversion'.[27] The church did not debate it at all. None of the five joined the church subsequently. The record simply states; 'The Holy Spirit had been working in our midst. "Follow Me," said Jesus.' [28]

One of those who followed Jesus in baptism that night was a newly qualified Scottish doctor, William Brewitt (Bill) Young, MB, BCh. He was the junior resident medical officer at nearby Mildmay Hospital and a Scotland international rugby player. He was only there at the time because his position had been upgraded by the Executive Committee of the hospital in 1941 so he could remain in position and not be called up.[29] In autumn 1942 he went, 'keen and energetic', to serve with the African Inland Mission in the Kerio Valley, Kenya with the Marakwet people. He worked at the Kapsowar Mission Hospital where he trained many nurses and assisted in the building of the local church.[30] He pleaded for more respect towards the local culture and requested that the word 'degraded' to describe it be erased from mission records.[31]

Young had been in the Scotland rugby team which won the Triple Crown in 1938. Home on leave from Africa in 1948 he was asked to play again and scored the winning try to beat England at Twickenham. An apparent sudden decision to be baptized at Shoreditch led him into years of effective Christian discipleship as 'a man of rich humour, devout faith and generous spirit'.[32]

But Clifford was taken seriously ill that night.

> I travelled home very cheered. I retired to bed at 10.30 and after 10 minutes I had a violent pain at the back of the head. Then I was seized with a trembling. I felt sure the end had come. Mrs Clifford phoned for the Doctor. He said it was a nervous breakdown. He called every day for a week and ordered me to rest for three months.[33]

Thirteen years of unbroken service in Shoreditch and the stress of the war years had taken its toll. But the church gave him time to recover and he returned to work in September with fresh enthusiasm.

The war turned. Victory was finally in sight and the Allies stormed the Normandy beaches. Then on the morning of 13th June, 1944 the first new pilotless bomb, the unnerving V-1 arrived.

One of them finally sealed the fate of Cuff's Tabernacle.

Chapter 12

Adjusting to a Changed Future

Sister Marjorie (Howden) arrived at Shoreditch in August, 1944 to a warm welcome. At her first Sunday evening service she was struck by how lovely the Tabernacle was: 'the dark pews, the open Baptistry, the beautiful windows through which light streamed, and the benediction of the sun resting on the worshippers'.[1]

Two days later on Tuesday, August 22nd a V-1 flying bomb dropped in Calvert Avenue near St Leonard's parish church. The School Hall and its rooms were damaged by the loss of some windows, ceilings and the glass skylights only recently repaired after the 1940 fire bombs. After further emergency repair these rooms were usable. The church on the other hand suffered considerably. All the windows and frames were blown out and doors damaged.

Ruth Clifford records the response of the members.

> All the windows blew in. Doors were ripped, ceilings dropped. Our hearts sank when we saw the state of it all. Very soon, the women, the men and the young people came. Could they help? One said, 'You always come to us when we are in trouble, so now we have come to you'. They all set to work with a will. Broken glass, window frames, plaster - all was cleared up. By nightfall it was difficult to imagine that the Church could have been in such a state. Our next task was where could we hold our Sunday services? Every hall and room had suffered. The Cartwright Hall was the most presentable. So it was scrubbed – the chairs washed - blue curtains, taken from the Church, were hung in the hall - a table and piano polished - a vase of flowers, and we had our church. The Margaret Lofts Hall was in a very bad state, but willing hands boarded the windows and swept up the debris, and so we had a meeting place for the children.[2]

However, the worst damage was unseen. The immense blast of one tonne of High Explosive had shaken the foundations and 'two main trusses had broken'.[3] The building would never be safe again for services. Access was only allowed from Hackney Road through the side entrances. Baptisms and marriages took place in the pulpit area, protected from falling masonry by a wooden covering and only as many present as could sit safe under the gallery.[4] For almost 20 years the services were held in the Lecture Hall. Ironically the fourteen year debt incurred by its restoration was finally cleared that November in a last effort which raised 4000 half-crowns.[5] One of the last to be baptised by Ernest Clifford in the Tabernacle baptistry at his final service on Sunday 16th February, 1947, was his own son, David. The record states 'our pastor was deeply moved.'

Promises were forthcoming of War Damage money. Some had already been paid from the loss of the Queen's Road 'chattels'. A section of members were eager to restore the Tabernacle, but wiser heads saw that there was no hope except to pull it down and build a new church.

One sorry aspect of the management of the church came to an end over this period. The three houses in Austin Street which the church owned had been a financial liability for decades. The original meagre rents hardly covered the cost of maintenance. Number 33, which had been condemned and empty for ten years, was finally pulled down in 1943. The other two houses were in disrepair and still costing the church. The deacons had clung on to them in spite of an offer in 1937 from the London County Council to buy them.[6] The German bombs put an end to any plans, however, and the remaining two houses were demolished in 1946. War Damage money was not available since the houses had been condemned or were worthless.[7] The land was still owned by the church in 1954, because of which it was liable for continuing costs concerning the drains.

The war ended. Ernest Clifford was anticipating the end of his ministry at Shoreditch. He had seen the church through demanding and difficult years with considerable wisdom and determination. He began to reframe the expectations of the church to help them adjust to a new future. He obtained agreement for women deacons to be co-opted onto the diaconate. Also it was agreed that the Senior Deaconess should attend and that Mrs Ruth Clifford would be welcome at their meetings. He proposed that the 'United (or Central) Committee' was established again to manage the transition, consisting of deacons of the church and representatives of the London Baptist Association and the Baptist Union.[8] It was hardly needed, since Clifford remained to serve until the arrival of his successor.

However, a wider radical plan was being hatched for a 'Federation of East London Churches' to combine the strengths of a number of churches. Rev Geoffrey King, pastor of the East London Tabernacle was to be the superintendent of a team of ministers serving East London Tabernacle, Mare Street Baptist Chapel, Victoria Park and Queensbridge Road, with Shoreditch Tabernacle as the base and preaching centre. An advisory board of LBA and BU members, with representatives of each church, would be formed. Finance would be pooled in a central fund. King preferred to make East London Tabernacle the base, but in principle the Shoreditch deacons agreed to the plan. At a subsequent Members Meeting significant leaders spoke for the motion, 'no questions were asked' and the meeting voted for it unanimously.[9] The clear-sighted church secretary Will Symons was the only opponent to this plan and he wrote to say he would resign if it went ahead. The whole idea soon died. It seems that the other local churches were not prepared to submit their independence to such a risky joint venture.

Clifford turned 65 in April 1946 and was eager to retire as soon as he could. He had never owned a car and the church did not have a manse for the minister. He encouraged the Church to buy a manse and soon 9, Forest Drive East, Leytonstone was bought with the help of a £700 loan from the Baptist Union Corporation and individual interest free loans.[10] He was to move from the district in November to his new home at Woburn Sands, but he did not wish the church to have a long interval without a pastor. He indicated that he was willing to come back on a reduced stipend to serve on Sundays and at midweek services until a new minister was appointed. He also would continue administration concerning 'appeals' and assist the church in finding a successor. The church eagerly agreed.[11]

The achievement of Ruth and Ernest Clifford at Shoreditch Baptist Church is later summed up as 'the recovery of an almost derelict church with a great past to become a living centre of Christian witness in peace and was the fruit of their joint ministry'.[12] The membership when he retired was 288, almost the same as in 1929 when he began. The considerable losses through movement of people out of London, the disruption of the war years and members' deaths had been answered by a constant stream of conversions, baptisms and inward transfers. The value of Clifford's work and the affection and high regard in which he and Ruth Clifford were held, summed up in a tribute by the church members on his retirement, can hardly be better expressed.

> This Church desires to put on record its profound thanks to Almighty God for having allowed us the privilege of having as our Pastor for eighteen years the Rev Ernest Clifford, MA, HCF, and our sincere thanks to him for all his faithful service, in which he was ably helped by his wife Mrs Clifford. His intense faith in God, his faithful preaching and courageous optimism – his splendid organising ability and sympathetic

consideration of others, especially during the war years when he was willing to share the dangers and give a helping hand, have left an indelible mark on many who would rise up and call him Blessed and would say, 'Well done good and faithful servant'.[13]

Clifford had told the deacons that 'a younger man was needed' to succeed him.[14] They began to look with all urgency and very soon settled on Rev. Harry Weston.

Chapter 13

Sowing so as to Reap

Wilfred Harold (Harry) Weston visited Shoreditch and preached on Sunday 27th October 1946. The deacons were impressed. With encouragement from their advisors and from members of the church who had written, they agreed unanimously to invite him to preach with a view to the pastorate, which he did on 8th December. The members met two weeks later and invited Weston to move from his ministry in Earl Shilton, Leicester to be pastor at Shoreditch for an initial three years. He wrote to S. F. Hudson, the church secretary,

> I am sure that many prayers have been offered and that God has made his will known. I myself have prayed and pondered over the matter and I can now say that whereas at first I was hesitant I now feel disposed to accept the call. What else can I do, believing that God is leading?

There was a mere few weeks between the final resignation of Ernest Clifford and Weston's arrival. His first service was Easter Sunday morning 1947, in the Lecture Hall, suitably decorated with flowers.[1] He was inducted on Saturday, May 3rd; 'a great day in the history of our

Lilian and Harry Weston

church'. Three hundred sat down to tea, including seventy from Earl Shilton. Sydney G. Morris, a well-known London Baptist minister and former Metropolitan Superintendent, preached and led the induction. A very useful £121 thank offering was given over the weekend.[2]

Weston immediately set to work. The church *Newsletter*, 'being the Magazine of Shoreditch Tabernacle Baptist Church', was revived and the first edition of 500 was printed in September to be followed up by another 1200. It was edited by Leslie Brown and a subscription of 2d per issue was asked after the first free issue. Money was at last promised from the War Damages Commission and urgent repair work on the Lecture Hall began.[3] The new manse in Leytonstone was purchased by the Baptist Union Corporation and Harry and Lillian Weston took possession in August.[4] Its disadvantage was that it placed the home of the minister well out of the immediate area of the church. Over following years this fact touched sensitivities with more local church members.

In the wartime new deacons had been co-opted to replace those away, but in September a proper election was held and ten deacons were appointed or reappointed, including the three required women. Sidney F. Hudson became Church Secretary.[5] He was to serve until 1959. These faithful men and women, together with the deaconesses and Mr and Mrs Weston, made up a strong and gifted leadership. There were seventeen people present at the deacons meeting in February 1948 and such attendance was regular. A thorough clear-out of rubbish and unwanted items 'from all over the premises' was arranged. This was to be followed by decorating some rooms and finally a 'mop and broom brigade' organised by one of the women deacons, Miss Dorothy 'Dolly' Orange.[6] There was however 'a feeling of dismay' in the church, because the promised Government money was held up and strong representations were made while the work was delayed until August.[7]

The church was generally in good spirits, recovering from years of damage, both physical and emotional. The membership was 262 at the end of 1947 and 225 children and young people were attached to the Sunday School. The varied societies and the mission work had largely survived the war years. Reviewing 1947 Hudson reported 'progress in all activities', 'steady numerical increase' of the Sunday congregation meeting in the Lecture Hall and youth organisations in a 'healthy state'.[8] Weston writes of the great number of people 'who have the Tabernacle very much in their hearts' even if they are not local or active in the church. The devotion of past members which under God had kept Shoreditch Tabernacle 'alive though peril and storm' still sustained the church in spirit and in finance.[9] Through this wide range of donors, by

Weston's personal efforts and the dedication of the members the deficit for 1947 was only £45.

The church choirmaster at this time was Len Sayer, a senior school music teacher and a graduate of Trinity College of Music. He was a regular accompanist for the George Mitchell Choir and built an excellent church choir, frequently to win its class in the London Music Festival. It provided a source of young singers for the Billy Graham evangelistic meetings in the 1950s.[10] The Tab choir also sang on the BBC Light Programme in May 1956.[11]

The Queensbridge Road Mission, led by Sister Marjorie (Marjorie Lillian Howden, 1944-50) and now located in Pownall Road was 'on fire' for Christ, with Sunday services, activities for children, women and young people. But the perennial need and appeal for more workers continued.[12] Those who remembered this time recall that 'On Sunday evenings about 130 people would crowd into the Lecture Hall and the atmosphere at services was sincere and spiritual, with strong singing.'[13]

Sister Marjorie (Howden)

Many young people were brought to Christ and became members. Evans reports 'in the first ten years of Harry Weston's ministry he baptised 86 people, most of them teenagers'. These were discipled and kept strong through the Boys' and Girls' Brigades, in youth groups and by a lively Sunday School. One of them was Edwin (later known as Ted) Hale. He was adopted by the Hales, a Tab family, and was also loved and encouraged by Harry Weston who baptised him. He went later to Rawdon College and became a Baptist minister.

Christian education was a particular concern and Weston introduced new developments in Sunday School with such effective teaching that people came to Shoreditch to see how it was done. Teachers had to attend Sunday worship and training on Mondays if they expected to teach their class on Sunday afternoon. They were also expected to attend special courses. Many of those trained like this went on to serve in other places. Another boy from this period who entered the Baptist ministry was Bill Mumby.

Weston gained great respect as a man of prayer and sincerity and he took his ministry very seriously. Of wide sympathy, he trained some of his leaders in praying for healing and introduced the midweek meeting to contemplative meditation. His pastoral method was to locate himself every day in the church building, looking in on the many activities, fully available till late in the evening for anyone in pastoral need, although some would have preferred proactive and regular pastoral visiting.

There were therefore challenges arising from the change of pastor. Tucked away in a final minute in February 1948 the deacons note 'a critical atmosphere abounding in some quarters'. Weston called them to face up to the difficulties then led special prayer for 'tact and guidance'.[14] One minor criticism was over the 'vesper'. The same short verse of a hymn was often sung at the end of meetings and services. John Shorey asked if a new vesper could be used on Sunday Evenings, as 'the present one was getting aged'. The pastor was very much in charge of the content of Sunday services and could respond without further consultation. Weston agreed to change it at once. He was also in charge of the subjects for the preaching and the choice of preachers. At the same meeting Mr R. Kirby passed on the view of several that the 'Good Friday Service preacher was not acceptable'. Weston 'took note of the complaint'.[15]

R. E. Pearson J.P. (1874-1948)

One significant event at this time was the death on February 12th 1948 of Richard Edward Pearson, J.P., at the age of 73. He is one of many unremembered influential laymen and women of Baptist life; 'the poor bay who became Mayor'.[16] He was converted under the ministry of William Cuff and baptised at the age of sixteen on 1st January 1891. He was a member of the church for 56 years and a deacon for 26. In particular he devoted himself to Sunday School work and the Gibraltar Walk mission just off Bethnal Green Road, 'the senior of the Tabernacle missions'[17] run in a former Congregational church. He led the Tabernacle choir for a number of years, helped in leading services, took weddings and funerals and assisted the pastors 'in every way'.

Richard and Ellen Pearson

He was for a time responsible for the open air work of the church and was often away from church duties on preaching trips, or for charity work. He was a respected deacon, rarely absent from the meetings, though he never pushed himself or his opinions. The Pearson's house was destroyed by 'enemy action' on May 10th 1941 and all their furniture was burned, but he and his wife Ellen stayed nearby and continued their service uninterrupted. He was always the first choice for chairman when the pastor was absent. He became president of the Baptist Lay-preachers' Association and of the Sunday School Union.

He worked all his life for the Royal London Friendly Society, becoming a District Superintendent. Like many free-church people of this time, 'believing in the value of Christian citizenship he took a great part in the work of Bethnal Green Borough'. He was a Justice of the Peace, serving as a magistrate for a number of years. He was twice elected as a liberal to the London County Council in the Bethnal Green division and became Mayor in 1930. In this role he followed his friend, Charles Fox, J.P., son of William Fox, the local chemist who founded Gibraltar Walk mission (combined in 1911 with the Old Nichol Street Mission). Charles continued his father's work and support. There was thus a deep connection between Pearson and Fox through their mission work and their political activities.

Richard E. Pearson

A very large congregation at his funeral included directors of the Royal London Assurance Company, Borough Councillors and the Mayor of Bethnal Green. The tribute to Pearson concludes,

> In all departments of life he never spared himself and was willing to spend and be spent in the service of his Master. Many have been blessed through his life and service and his messages and generous help will be missed by us all.'[18]

The good work and spiritual influence of such a man cannot be measured.

The 'Ladies Hall' was soon renamed, and it still is, 'The Richard Pearson Hall'.

The issue which dominated the church in the 1950s was, naturally, the question of the repair, or replacement, of Cuff's Tabernacle. There was delay in the arrival of the promised War Damage funds. It was soon decided that the Tabernacle could not be repaired. A new building entirely was needed. Some voices favoured closing the church entirely and moving the congregation into the suburbs. This was soon dismissed. The leaders were still deeply committed to Shoreditch and its local people.

An event 'without precedent in the history of our church' took place in 1951 when Sidney Hudson married fellow deacon Dorothy 'Dolly' Orange. This raised great amusement since she was Captain of the Girls' Brigade and they also were respectively Church Secretary and deacon.

An evangelistic 'campaign' with five young Bristol Baptist College students was held in the summer of that year, including local house to house visiting and open air preaching. It ended with seven young people being baptised. These included Len Hitchman, a deacon's son, and Weston's own son David, who was to serve as Church Secretary from 1971 to 1995.

Financial stability was a continuing problem. The whole area was changing and many streets of small inadequate houses were replaced with flats. In spite of Weston's pleading for them to remain, younger members married and moved out to the suburbs and were lost to the area and the church. However, David and Joyce Weston and Ken and Ena Jones and others remained and 'carried much of the burden, with Roy Fouracre, over the difficult years from the early sixties'.[19] The regular income was not sufficient and Harry Weston appealed each year for renewed effort. Mrs Lillian Weston acted as his personal assistant and was formally thanked 'for all her help in typing and secretarial work'.[20] At the end of three years, with a 'hearty commendation' from the deacons, the members voted unanimously for him to continue permanently with an increase in stipend.[21] But in March 1951 income 'showed decrease in most items'.[22]

During this difficult time of transition the church was still active and productive. There was a 'deep stirring among the young and "very young" people'.[23] Keith Sobey was sent to Shoreditch in 1953 by the Spurgeon's College Council to assist Weston in a 'pre-collegiate year'. He took up many ministerial duties, including preaching at the services in the Lecture Hall, 'full in the evenings, more so than the mornings.' Joan Mariner, with her brother and sister, had been in the church for some years. She was active in the Youth Work, a teacher in the Sunday School and then its secretary. Sobey tells how they fell in love, but neither said anything for the whole sixteen months. Then, on the very day of his final service before leaving, they met alone in the 'quiet room'. She wanted to take a photo; he had a book to give her. There was a hug... ... and that was that! They were married in 1958 after Keith finished his training.[24]

William (Bill) Mumby, a former labourer and timber porter for Shoreditch Borough Council and a long standing worker among the children and youth, was also commended by the church for Baptist ministry in January 1959. He trained at Rawdon Baptist College and was ordained in the Lecture Hall in 1963. A few weeks later he married Joyce Hitchman, a trained musician from a prominent church family. Kathleen Woodbridge (later Mills) was commended for Deaconess training at the same time.[25]

The deaconesses, supported by Lillian Weston, ran the still flourishing women's work. Raymond Brown, later to be Principal of Spurgeon's College, was one of a series of first year students allocated to speak at a midweek Women's Meeting in 1952. This was considered hard service by the chosen student, but he recalls a lively atmosphere and much spiritual benefit.[26] At this time the church also had a second women's meeting, run by Carrie Cheesman. It was the old Queen's Road mission meeting which had been bombed out of their buildings. They successfully served a different kind of East End woman.

A 'most remarkable lady' was Miss Agnes Perkins, 'Aggie' to a favoured few. She had a wooden leg and 'was greatly loved in the church, austere on the surface, but blazing warm on the inside'. She lived in Dalston and looked after her frail mother and her father, a piece-work docker often unemployed. Agnes appears in the records as leader of the girls' Sunday Bible class and then joint leader with George Hitchman of the mixed Senior Bible Class. For many years she was the person who acted as agent to sell the *Baptist Times*. She was clearly a shrewd operator, since among the continual church deficits, this little fund always made a slight profit. 'She was instrumental in Joan Mariner's conversion and was thrilled to be able to say that a member of her Bible class had married a minister.'[27]

George Benjamin (G. B.) Cartwright, the long-serving and able deacon and church treasurer, died in January 1957. Baptised by William Cuff at the age of 15, he had been a 'most devoted servant' for 60 years, deacon for 40 years, and Sunday School Superintendent and treasurer for 30 years. He followed his honoured father George as responsible for the finances of the church as well as working in the family timber merchants. He is another example of deeply committed and able believers who served Christ in Shoreditch Baptist Church, 'sparing not himself, nor his time, nor his substance.'[28]

A team of students from the John Clifford Society, which brought together Baptist students in London, came to Shoreditch in September

1960 for a 'campaign', in particular to visit in the newly built Dorset Estate, Diss Street. The report notes 1156 homes visited, some more than once, and 652 interviews with people 'willing to discuss religion'.[29] A prior visit of three students to take a service included Faith Clark, who spoke from a pulpit for the first time at Shoreditch. She notes that 'by the next summer vacation I was taking services, on my own, around the Gloucestershire village churches, but Shoreditch was where I first put my toe in the water in a church service…. .. I am sure that a kindly congregation gave us confidence to do more.'[30] Faith Bowers, as she became after marriage, is still active in Baptist life writing on Baptist history and other subjects, most notably on disability issues.

The rebuilding project occupied the church. The first plan was far too expensive. A more modest idea, soon rejected, was to build a new church inside the old Tabernacle.[31] A further thought was to flatten everything, including the Lecture Hall, sell some land and fund a smaller new building. However, after a change of architect, further delays over War Damage funding and the Tabernacle 'condemned as unsafe', all interested parties agreed it should be 'demolished as soon as possible' and a more suitable building erected in its place. Of the 73 present in November 1954 at the members' meeting only two dissented from this decision.[32]

The pews now in East London Tabernacle

The loss of the Tabernacle rooms and the building work itself, presented great difficulties. The transition, which took nine years, was very stressful to Weston and the leadership, as well as a sad time for many. The timber pews were sold to the East London Tabernacle for £650. They were unscrewed and put together again in their new home. You can go there and sit in them to this this day or see them on that church's website.[33]

The very worthy pipe organ, built for Cuff in 1905, was sold for £1150 to another church which had been destroyed by bombing, Holy Trinity, Hounslow, where it is still in use. An electric organ was bought ready for the new church.[34] A baptistry was needed in the Lecture Hall and fabric deacon John Shorey installed a tank under the stage area.[35] Used for the first time in April 1956, 'it was made of iron with sharp edges and quite a health hazard ... ... hastily made and built in'. It was only removed in 2008.[36] Some present members were baptised in it including, on 19th May 1959, Vi Julier's father who had responded during the Billy Graham 'relay' from Glasgow.

In May 1960 the Lea Bridge Demolition Company of Edmonton began their work. It was completed by November. Carrie Cheesman the caretaker was ill in the chapel keeper's cottage. She had her bed turned round so she could see the old Tabernacle being demolished. Useful material was sold off, but every day a big fire was fuelled by matter taken from the Tabernacle.[37] Terry Jellis, who still lives locally, well remembers the demolition since he was present when a bull-dozer tore down the walls. He recalls the men breaking the locks on the big front doors to get in and then saw lead from the roof being stripped off 'like rolls of carpet' before the bull-dozer could begin its dangerous work.[38]

The ground was soon clear for a new Tabernacle.

The Tabernacle 1960

Chapter 14

Loved for What Happened Inside

There were more planning delays. The London County Council did not like aspects of the building plans for the new church. These were adjusted and finally agreed in November 1961, with a small exchange of land for which the church would receive £1180. The first builder's tender was thought too high and help was sought from Sir Cyril Black MP, a wealthy Baptist in the property business. His surveyor found ways of reducing the cost, but in the end not by much. In spite of repeated efforts to economise, the final bill was £30,693.[39] Most of the funding was eventually to come from the War Damages Commission, from money 'ported' from the destroyed Queen's Road building and from the sale of Pownall Road. Gifts and legacies made up the rest.[40] Supervising the project, after a change from architect Norman Webster, was John Ainsworth and the chosen builders were Goddard & Phillips of Highgate.[41]

The work began on 18th March 1962. A stone-laying ceremony was organised for 22nd June and planned to include young people and 'a coloured child if possible'.[42] Miss E. Fallows 'the senior member' laid the stone, witnessed by the mayors of Bethnal Green and Shoreditch. Also present was Frederick G. Woolvett, with long connections to the church and owner of M. Perkins & Son, Trimming Maker. The Rev Geoffrey Hayden, General Superintendent of the Metropolitan Area, presided.[43]

The Perkins, Crisp and Woolvett Trimming Makers

It is worth pausing to relate the long links of the Perkins, Crisp and Woolvett families with Shoreditch and its Baptist Church. The house in Curtain Road where the first Baptist group met in 1829 was the home of William Perkins, Trimming Maker (1780 – 1851). His daughter-in-law Mary, widowed early, developed the Trimmings business which continues to this day as M. Perkins & Son. Her son, another William Perkins (1843-1924) was baptised by Cuff and was member of the church. After six days of work in the business 'Sunday was spent at Chapel', so it is not surprising that he appears in a number of places in the records offering support or finance, as do other members of the family. William went to school with James C. Crisp (1840-1927) who was a child in Providence Hall, Cumberland Street. He made the drawing of the first church building, Providence Chapel. The Crisp family also feature widely in the records. His father (also James Crisp) had a Gentleman's Taylors in Hackney Road and when they went out of business, J. C. Crisp joined William Perkins in the trimmings business, becoming the commercial traveller for the firm. He served as Sunday School secretary for 65 years; a man of 'quiet unobtrusiveness and gracious courtesy'.[44]

After their deaths the business was sold to Crisp's son-in-law, Fred G. Woolvett and the family still own the business, now under the direction of Fred's great grandson Matthew Woolvett. The company is no longer located in Shoreditch. But the beautiful tassels and trimmings which surrounded the first small group of Baptists in 61 Curtain Road at their meeting in 1829 are still made by M. Perkins and Son.[45]

William Perkins (1843-1924) and J. C Crisp (c. 1844 – 1924)

After eighteen years of waiting and eighteen months of building, on Saturday, 14th December, 1963 Mr. Ralph McCombie, a regular supporter of the church, officially opened the door of the new Tabernacle. In use for over 50 years it was loved for what happened inside rather that for its appearance. Externally the building was typical of its time and type; 'a very low key post war building which replaced a grand 19th Century church'. Set back from the road, it was later judged, by its architecture, and its positioning in a designated conservation area, to be 'undistinguished'.[46]

The inside of the building was more impressive and was thoughtfully arranged. It would seat 300 people in wooden pews. There was an open baptistry, a central aisle and side aisles. The front of the interior 'was intended to convey the message of the "Risen Lord"'.[47] Many individuals contributed to the furnishings. The communion table was a gift from Miss Lilah French. The pulpit was made of wood from the old Tabernacle pulpit by Mr Robson, of a prominent church family. Ernest and Ruth Clifford gave money for the reading lectern.[48] The Cuff family asked to be responsible for the interior of the minister's vestry, in memory of William Cuff.[49]

Many former members and invited guests came to the opening, including the Mayor of Shoreditch, Rev Meredith Davies and the Mayor of Bethnal Green, Robert Rosamund. Harry Weston led the dedication service and the speaker was Geoffrey Hayden, London Baptist Superintendent. There was a further evening meeting and then at 11.00 the next morning Harry Weston led the first Communion Service in the church he had seen built. Sir Cyril Black preached at the evening service. It was a weekend of great celebration. Violet Julier was in charge of the cakes.[50]

After the enormous effort and time taken to see through the project, it is not surprising that Weston was ill and exhausted. He had earlier developed diabetes and, according to Sister Elsie (Elsie Drewett, 1959-68) 'ate all the wrong things' at nearby cafés. It was announced, on the suggestion of Hayden, that 'the pastor would be taking a rest after the opening' of the new building.[51] His ministry in Shoreditch was coming to an end. The Divine Healing Mission had approached him in 1959. They now renewed the invitation for him to become the full time free-church chaplain at their centre in Crowhurst.

Weston was well suited to this position and the offer matched his long interest in Christian healing. He was a sensitive and complex person with a deep concern for people in personal and mental distress. It had been a particular strength of his ministry and many were greatly helped by his pastoral and counselling skills. He told the deacons in June 1964 that 'he felt led after much thought and prayer to terminate his ministry' in September and move to Crowhurst. 'Overall the church ow[ed] Harry Weston an enormous debt for seventeen years hard labour, with much to discourage him. He saw the church through to the new building and laid firm foundations on the way.'[52] The church appointed Henry Bryant of Vernon, Kings Cross as moderator and began to seek a new minister.

There was a further attempt at this time to create 'some kind of federation of inner London churches'. The London Baptist Association had an offer of help from the London County Council for 75% of the cost to support church leaders in key locations. The Shoreditch deacons agreed in principle and some 'group' ministers' meetings, lay leaders' meetings and joint prayer and other services were held in the next few years. However, a formal federation with joint ministries was never put into action.[53] Finance continued to be an issue at Shoreditch. The building fund was still in debt when the new church opened and the final account in February 1965 shewed a deficit of £2,718.[54] To fund the general support of the church, loans were sought and appeals made for more committed giving.

Trainee deaconesses c. 1947. A young Elsie Drewett on the right

Elsie Drewett

During three years of interregnum the mainstay of the ministry was the deaconess, Elsie Drewett (1959-68), the very last in the long line of able and dedicated Tabernacle deaconesses. She was amply suited by background to the work at Shoreditch. Born into a large family in a poor part of London she fitted happily into the context. She was already an experienced church leader, trained as a young woman at Struan, the Deaconesses' College in Wimbledon Park. She went immediately from there into pastoral charge of the first 'initial pastorate' of the London Baptist Association at New Addington, Croydon in 1948.[55]

Shoreditch appointed her in September 1959 as a youth worker, half her stipend being paid by the local authority and the other half by Baptist Home Mission. At Shoreditch she engaged in many ministerial duties and did most of the pastoral visiting. When Harry Weston left, Elsie led the Bible Study and other mid-week meetings and preached occasionally. It was also agreed that she could administer the discretionary Communion Fund without consultation. She stayed throughout the interregnum and remained to enable the new minister to settle and begin his ministry and studies.

Elsie Drewett

She was a close friend of the hospitable Carrie Cheesman in the caretaker's cottage and took lunch breaks with this 'lovely woman'. She moved in 1968 to Henley in Arden, where she was in sole charge of the Baptist church and in 1975 was 'Rev'd up' as she called it; transferred with many other deaconesses to the accredited list of ordained Baptist ministers.[56] She was invited back to Shoreditch for many events and was the preacher at the Church Anniversary in 1982.

It speaks a great deal of her relationship with the church that on retirement in 1983 she returned to London and served the Tabernacle people for five more years.[57] Elsie lived with her mother in Tottenham and took the bus down to Shoreditch regularly. For a short while she was treasurer of the Women's Fellowship and helped to lead the church *Midsummer Festival* in June 1986.[58] The deacons noted her as a possible moderator in 1988.

The people looked on Elsie Drewett with great gratitude, later noting that she 'has been sustained in a wonderful way throughout the long period we were without a pastor'.[59] Elsie was the last Shoreditch deaconess and has been an exemplary, long-serving, dedicated and effective Baptist deaconess and Baptist minister.

Graduation group, Struan, 1947. Elsie Drewett, back left

The church considered a large number of possible ministers. Named at this time were Keith Sobey (mentioned earlier), Brian Treharne, Edmund Heddle, Brian Richards, Tom Neal, David Clarke, Arnold E Sewell, H. S. Tymms, E. J. Ridout, David L. Jones and a young David Beer, returned from a year in Louisville, Kentucky after leaving Spurgeon's College. Most declined outright, some visited and then declined; the church became very discouraged.[60] Shoreditch was a tough calling.

Finally the moderator offered the name of Gordon P. Giller. He had been Assistant Manager of Goddard and Phillips, the builders for the new chapel, so he knew the church. A lay preacher for many years he was now entering full time ministry.[61] He led worship and preached in the church on 25th February 1967 with a view to the pastorate. The deacons were unanimous. Giller accepted the invitation of the church and was inducted on 9th September. He was a friendly, welcoming man who made good relationships with both adults and children and was much appreciated by the people. The Baptist Union had agreed that suitable people could pastor a church and at the same time study and prepare for Baptist accreditation. So Giller began the required six years of study under a tutor while serving at Shoreditch.

Chapter 15

Social Change and Political Action

Gordon Giller's appointment was intended to be a 'group ministry' with other nearby Baptist churches; the *North East London Fellowship of Churches*. This consisted eventually of four nearby 'inner London' Baptist churches: Vernon Kings Cross, The Downs, Clapton (now Open Doors Baptist Church), Dalston and Salters' Hall (now New River Baptist Church) and Shoreditch Tabernacle. This arrangement was agreed on the basis that 'no loss of identity' would result and operated in a limited way for a number of years.[62]

The pastoral and teaching ministry was never truly shared among the group, but a council of representatives arranged joint meetings, training days and evangelistic activities, including guest services and film evenings, using a new jointly owned film projector.[63] The most important contribution of the group ministry to Shoreditch was the appointment by agreement of all four churches of a Youth Leader, John Evans. His salary was paid by grants from the Inner London Education Authority (75%) and the Inner London Fund of the London Baptist Association (25%).[64] Evans served these churches from 1971-75, led the weekly open youth 'Club' at Shoreditch and assisted the church in other ways. In May 1972 there were 55 junior and 30 seniors recorded in the Club.[65] Criticism emerged of his active involvement however, since some thought his role was to be support, training and inspiration rather than running clubs in each of the churches.

Gordon Giller

A number of new initiatives were taking place as Giller arrived. Sister Elsie, with Joyce Hitchman, continued to be deeply engaged in youth and children's work. Elsie was well equipped for such work, because of her background and as one of eight children herself. She was on the 'Care Committee' of the nearby primary school at Columbia Road and followed up pastoral needs they referred to her. She headed up a successful mission in 1967 to which 116 children came, 38 of them 'with little or no religious backgrounds'. This effort led to increase in the Sunday School in all departments.[66] Missions for children at Easter or in September continued to be a feature of Giller's time and later. The afternoon Sunday School still attracted up to 100 children. It was moved, after a trial period, to the time of the morning service.[67]

A Missionary Council was formed to stimulate prayer and giving to overseas mission. David Weston, a deacon since 1956, had been encouraging the leadership to think creatively about the future, particularly with children and young people in mind and a Youth Council was formed. The 'Club' aimed at non-church young people began. It attracted a good number, although there was the usual 'trouble' with some boys. A careful review of the church roll was also taking place and 57 members were removed in July 1967, most for non-attendance. More were removed in the years that followed. The membership was 106 by 1970.[68]

Giller was good at encouraging practical help. Being a builder by trade, he saw what needed to be done in the old Lecture Hall buildings and organised it. In his time the Cheesmans' Caretaker's Cottage received its first bathroom and a permanently roofed-in kitchen. In an 'unfortunate accident' at a Girls' Brigade district parade one of the officers disappeared into the empty baptistry! So after serious debate, removable iron railings were placed round the open pool.[69]

The 1960s was the time of ecumenical enthusiasm as well as charismatic disturbance. Giller was very eager for co-operation with other churches. He was a founder, with the vicar of Hoxton Parish Church, of the Shoreditch Council of Churches and its chair in 1970.The church participated in joint Lent Bible study groups, combined services at Easter and the annual Christian Aid appeal. An informal Sing-in of *Messiah* at Hoxton Parish Church involved soloists and the congregation as the chorus, with a conductor to keep everyone together.[70]

The charismatic movement did not have much impact at Shoreditch. There was a move by 'a number of people' in 1966 for singing before the main evening service. After modest discussion this was agreed to be 'on a limited number of occasions'.[71] House groups and their 'pitfalls' were discussed and cautiously commended by the deacons, but no more is heard of them.[72]

There was considerable discouragement in this period. Significant long standing members died, such as Sidney F. Hudson the former church secretary.[73] Many others moved out of the fast changing area. A rare baptism and a small trickle of new members did not replace members the church was losing. Increasing social deprivation combined with substantial local redevelopment produced a sense of disruption and a lack of connection between the church and the community. Aware of this, a systematic visitation programme, with pairs of members going out, was kept up for two years.[74] The Youth work and the Boys' and Girls' Brigades continued to function well, albeit with gradually declining numbers. At the beginning of 1971 Giller urged members frankly to 'a change of heart'. He said that 'the fellowship had grown cold', that prayer meetings and Bible study times were badly attended and referred to 'difficult problems' in the last two years.[75]

David Weston

David Weston, now church secretary, summed up 1971 as 'another difficult year, with little progress to show for much hard work'. His report speaks of a 'very real crisis which is upon us', but urges members to be open to change, because the opportunities are great and 'the Lord's resources are without limit'. These calls seem not to have been fruitful. A year later Giller refers to 'prolonged lethargy' in the church and Weston to 'complacent fatalism'. The pastor later gave a 'stern word on gossip' under which the church was 'shocked and ashamed'.[76]

Financially the church was just about breaking even, but the improvement and maintenance of the Lecture Hall, as well as the manse, called endlessly for more money. Substantial loans were obtained at different times from the Baptist Building Fund and the John Bradford Trust.[77] While finding a minister's stipend and trying to keep up with growing national inflation there was little money available to repay them.

On a positive note, a significant change was happening in the church, mirroring wider social change. The first black members of the congregation were Gloria Daley and Beryl Rhoden. Gloria recalls being turned away at the church door, but pressed on in. Beryl, a Jamaican mother of three daughters had arrived in the district in 1962. She was 29 and the girls attended Columbia Road School. Beryl tells how they were tormented by the other children and recalls, 'when they would come in crying, we used to sit together and cry.' After the birth of one of her daughters, Margaret Foreman and Daisy Berry (later church treasurer) came to visit her. Beryl began to attend. Not everyone was receptive, but Beryl bore the rejections.[78] However, Gordon Giller welcomed her warmly and she applied for church membership. After a home visit with Mrs Giller and Miss L. Rogers and a course of instruction with the pastor, he baptised her on Sunday 6th December 1970.[79]

In 1972, after six years of ministry in Shoreditch and to the great sadness of the members, Gordon Giller left. The whole area was socially depressed and did not seem to have a future. The church was suffering from the lack of new and younger leaders and the mood was greatly affected by surrounding conditions. The Church entered six years without a minister. Margaret Jarman, minister of Dalston and Salters Hall, became the moderator. A succession of possible names for the pastorate was offered but, as before, the church was repeatedly turned down. The area and the church was an even less appealing proposition than eight years previously. Sunday evening services were led by visiting preachers. Sunday mornings were undertaken by Roy Fouracre the Treasurer and David Weston the Secretary, who took alternate months in an agreed pattern to give some consistency in the teaching. Numbers declined and the congregation on a bad day might be single figures.

The Sunday School, which met now at morning service time, was still drawing many children and they came into the service at the end for a final hymn and prayer. The Youth Club meeting weekly in the Lecture Hall was also in good heart, led at this time by Ena Jones, the Cheesmans' daughter. She was a local school dinner lady, a 'chubby and cheerful' energetic East Ender who took an active part in a number of activities.[80]

There seemed no immediate prospect of finding a pastor, so Margaret Jarman negotiated with Peter Manson at Spurgeon's College for a student. Derek Allan was offered as Student Pastor for a year from November 1975. He worked hard, bringing a measure of stability and giving 'new focus and enthusiasm' to the church.[81] He preached twice a month, initiated evangelistic work, started a monthly family service and led deacons and church meetings. Most significant, in November 1976 he organized a 'most encouraging' youth mission with some fellow students.

At this point two more Spurgeon's students enter the Shoreditch Tabernacle story. Paul and Lynda Henstock were involved in the youth mission and Lyn agreed to follow up those who responded. They were invited to succeed Derek Allan as student pastors. As Paul Henstock's college training concluded, a plan was constructed for a joint ministry for Shoreditch Tabernacle and

Lynda and Paul Henstock

Dalston and Salters' Hall with Paul and Lynda; the two of them, now both ordained ministers, serving the two churches. The Home Mission Fund was to grant £600 a year to be matched by the churches.

The Shoreditch members called them unanimously on 16th July 1978 and they were inducted together on Saturday October 6th.[82] Paul had been a chartered secretary (ACIS) and both had completed the BA theology degree at Spurgeon's. They took an active part in the pastoral ministry of both churches. Some joint events were organised, usually at Shoreditch. They lived in the Dalston church manse at 128, Winston Road, Stoke Newington. The Shoreditch manse was being rented.

They were greatly appreciated during their time as student pastors and ten years of ministry at Shoreditch. There were some initial setbacks. George Hitchman died in 1976 after 52 years' service in the Boys' Brigade as officer and captain. David Weston took over. Roy Fouracre, the longstanding deacon and treasurer, was developing Alzheimer's disease and very reluctantly gave up his active roles. There was continuing 'extraordinary expenditure on buildings and decorations' and tension over the pattern of Sunday morning services.[83] But the church began to steady.

Daisy Berry

The secretary's report for 1979 speaks of increasing numbers and a 'genuine quickening of the Holy Spirit'. The giving and the financial position improved, helped by a loan of £900 from a member. An able new treasurer was found in Miss Daisy Berry. She kept a tight rein on the expenditure and over the next few years there was increasing financial stability. It was decided quite soon to end Home Mission funding and repay other loans.[84] A 'One Step Forward' campaign was begun in 1981 and continued for a year, although the results were mixed. Stuart Davison came as student assistant pastor from Spurgeon's.

The caretaker's cottage became available on the retirement of Mrs Carrie Cheesman, who had been caretaker (at first with her husband) since 1945. In a last minute arrangement another Spurgeon's student, David Brownnutt, came with his wife Jane and their two small boys to live in the cottage rent free in return for caretaking duties (October 1981- July 1985). They became 'non-voting members' and David as 'pastoral assistant' was invited to attend deacons' meetings, adding considerably to the strength of the ministry team and preaching occasionally in both Shoreditch and Salters Hall.

Equally significant, Jane Brownnutt began a Mother and Toddlers Group which met in the small room under the gallery next to the entrance to the Lecture Hall. The first week there were only Jane and her son present, with the help of Julie Etheridge and Dorothy Davis (80 years old and willing to make the tea). Soon there were eight or more regular mothers and they also opened on a second morning of the week.[85] Dorothy turned out to be a brilliant listener and everyone's ideal grandma.[86] In all these positive developments, Weston concluded in January 1982 that 'the people continue to appreciate the services of Paul and Lyn as pastors'.[87]

There was also at this time a significant move over the Mildmay Hospital. A truly local, but independent Christian hospital for 100 years, it had been given, in the 1946 Health Act, the right to sustain its Christian and evangelistic foundation. In 1982, to the anger of the local community the Health Authority decided to close it. But dramatic events were to change that.

One night Jane Brownnutt attended a public meeting where this was being debated. She sent a message to David who was babysitting that local people, including members of Militant Tendency, were asking why the clergy were not present. David changed places with her and was soon deeply involved in the fight to save the hospital along with other objectors.

Clergy did get involved and they set up a committee in which David Brownnutt and Margaret Foreman, a deacon of the Tabernacle were key players. The deacons' vestry became their office and meeting place. They oganised a protest march from the hospital to Trafalgar Square where a well-known ex-convict, Fred Lemon, led a prayer, which started ' 'Ere God, bless Mildmay...' A large banner for the march was made on the wide floor of the Lecture Hall.[88] Also in the action group was Helen Taylor-Thompson, chair of the Mildmay board, married to an influential civil servant. She mobilised wide support and a charitable trust was set up to run the hospital, charging the Health Authority for services.

Margaret Foreman

What were the services like in the 1980s? The Sunday morning service was at 11.00, one hour long. In 1969 during Giller's ministry the afternoon Sunday School had been moved, after a trial period, to the morning service time. At the end of the sermon a hymn was sung and an electric bell was rung to summon the children and teachers into church. One Sunday a month there was a communion service at 10.30 for 20 minutes; 'as simple as possible'. One deacon served both bread and wine, with one thanksgiving prayer by the leader and one hymn. This was followed by a short break when the bulk of the congregation arrived. At 11.00 the normal worship began, until at precisely 11.45 the children entered.[89] This practice continued for over 20 years. A paper (probably from 1985) for the eleven o'clock service gives more detail to visiting preachers.[90]

SHOREDITCH TABERNACLE – MORNING SERVICE OUTLINE

11.00 Call to worship
HYMN
Scripture Reading (often Responsive or Unison)
Prayers of intercession and Lord's Prayer
HYMN

11.45 Offering - RING BELL to summon Sunday School.
The offering is taken up at this point, but not brought forward till Sunday School have arrived.

Notices - given by Ch. Sec. David Weston, after which Sunday School come in - Seniors, Juniors, Beginners and Crèche.
When all assembled, Sunday School representatives and adult steward bring offerings forward. (Call them to do this.)

Dedication of offerings.
A word to the children and Y.P. We don't give a 'children's talk' in order not to detract from the lesson they have just had, but often a comment on something of topical relevance.
HYMN

12.00 Benediction.

The instruction tells the preacher that the church uses the *Baptist Hymn Book*, *Mission Praise* and *Youth Praise*. Eurannie Afuwape is named as the organist, though it unkindly says she is 'not ever so proficient and is more confident with BHB than with the newer items.' However, she will practise if given the music a few days before. There is no open prayer because the 'acoustics of the building means they are usually inaudible!' The preacher may ask for suggestions to be incorporated in a led prayer. Good News Bibles were available in the pews.

The pattern for monthly Sunday morning communion created a fair amount of difficulty over a number of years. The arrangement began in 1969, when the Sunday School classes moved to the morning. Numbers at the 10.30 communion gradually decreased and the careful instruction needed for visitors illustrates the problems created. The service became less and less effective. It 'did not really work', with a small number of people sitting separated in the pews. Over the next 20 years the proposal was made a number of times to move the communion into the 11.00 a.m. service. It was always defeated at the deacons' meeting and voted against by most members. There was clearly a strong difference of opinion over this tradition and after one such occasion it was recorded that David Brownnutt 'is not happy with this decision'. It was not until January 1991 that the communion became part of the morning service.'[91]

The bad acoustics of the 1963 building with its high roof was also an ongoing saga. Derek Allan recalled baptizing one woman who made the common mistake of not closing her mouth fully when being immersed. She came up out of the water with a loud gasp for air that echoed round the roof for a few seconds to the brief consternation of the congregation.[92] There were repeated efforts to improve the sound with different public address systems. It was not helped by a 1982 break-in, when microphones and leads were stolen, and then a more damaging robbery in 1986. The windows were replaced with double glazing in 1981, which helped reduce traffic noise.[93] The acoustic difficulties were a major problem as long as the 1963 building stood and no speaker system seemed to solve it. Hugh Doyle, the pastor in 1992, suggested that the best thing was not to use it at all!

The older buildings needed continual maintenance. They were structurally unsound and Paul Henstock called in a surveyor who said he 'did not expect a very extended life of the Lecture Hall block'. Props were needed in the beginners' room to hold up the roof. Weston later concluded that the 'Lecture Hall block was approaching the end of its useful life'.[94] In 1991 large timber baulks were put in place to hold up the external wall behind the caretaker's cottage.[95]

The church was led by a small group of about seven dedicated leaders and twelve other members who regularly attended church business meetings. It was hard to sustain the various historic church organisations, although they functioned well. The Boys' and Girls' Brigades ran effectively as did the Youth meetings, the Sunday school and the Women's work. Evangelistic efforts were made, including a youth mission in August 1984, and visitation was organised from time to time, both to new houses and to needy members.

A student from Spurgeon's College, David V. Evans, came as student pastor from January 1985 for one year. That same year the church celebrated its 150th anniversary, the founding having been agreed as 1835. A committee was formed to set up anniversary events, including a retreat day in March with Rev. Arthur Thompson, the Metropolitan Area Superintendent, and a weekend celebration in October with a newly formed choir. Celebration mugs were produced. On an October Saturday 230 people attended a service and most stayed for tea. The Sunday was well attended and was 'a time of happy fellowship and reunion.'

Evans was commissioned to write a history of the church.[96] His well-researched and illuminating booklet entitled *More Light, More Power*, after the Shoreditch Borough motto, has provided a valuable basis for the present history. So Evans' good influence, as well as his interest in the church, has continued far longer than his year as a student pastor. Other students came and commended themselves to the people and gave further help: Clifford Taylor (summer 1985), Jonathan Calvert (1986)

Paul and Lynda Henstock and their two boys in 1985 with Agnes Salmon, the oldest member.

and Edward Pillar (1987).[97]

The Henstock's sons were born and Lynda then transferred to the Baptist Union supplementary ministry list, assisting where she could. In 1988 Paul and Lynda were accepted by the Baptist Missionary Society for short term mission and left Shoreditch to pastor the Baptist Church at Cinnamon Gardens, in Colombo, Sri Lanka. Their ten years of committed ministry and godly influence in the church (and at Salters Hall) had been greatly appreciated. Paul was described as 'always gentle, friendly, supportive, pastoral and strong'[98] and the judgement of the members was that 'they had left the church in good heart'.[99]

Chapter 16

Land and Love in Action

The character of the church had been gradually changing during the 1980s, so had the surrounding context. The racial mix of the congregation altered and church activities were evolving. Immigrant churches and other groups needed places to meet; increasing pressure to develop the buildings was felt by the church and by its neighbour, the Christian foundation Mildmay Hospital; land was now immensely valuable in London, adding extra tension to any change or use of space; the 60 member church, with 40 in regular Sunday attendance, found it difficult to supply leaders for the organisations and closures were inevitable. The financial position of the church was generally steady, but the leaders and denominational advisors recognized that further membership decline would mean the church would be unable to pay a minister without help from outside. On the positive side, a trickle of baptisms and new members kept the church encouraged and outward looking mission was continually in mind.

In 1982 a Bangladeshi school began to rent rooms in the Lecture Hall for £500 a year. The income was very helpful to the church, but the usual difficulties soon arose over damage to property and access. Then it was discovered that the school was run by a Muslim group and that Islam had been taught.[1] This matter was soon resolved, under threat of terminating the agreement, but irregular payment of rent was a continuing issue. Other groups and organisations also applied to hire the valuable space of the Church and Lecture Hall. New Pentecostal churches applied to hire the building, but this was allowed only for a single baptism service, which filled the church. In 1992 a Zairian church, *Église de Dieu*, started to hold services in French on Sunday afternoons. This was a happy relationship, largely enriching for the Tabernacle people.[2] The same year a local playgroup moved into the Hall under the leadership of Anita Fanni.[3]

As the racial mix and attitudes of the congregation changed, the image of the great church that used to be gradually had to alter. Noise before services troubled the deacons and late attendance to morning worship was 'deplored' by some. More seriously, the Girls' Brigade company closed in 1988, Mrs Joyce Weston having retired as captain.[4] The Boys' Brigade also declined and by 1990, with only two on the register, it also closed after nearly 60 years. Ecumenical relationships grew through occasions of shared worship with the Parish Church of St Leonard's and joint groups during Lent. Some regular members of the congregation had not been baptised as believers. It was argued in 1989 that such people might 'make a valuable contribution' to the leadership and management of the church. After thoughtful debate the church meeting voted by a large majority to create an Associate Member list.[5]

However, the most significant challenge of the 1980s and beyond was the development of the church buildings. Two factors dominated this debate for the next 30 years. The first was over the piece of land bordering Hackney Road in front of the 1963 building; the 'frontage'. The second was the proximity of the Mildmay Hospital.

On request of the Greater London Council, the church and the trustees of the property, the Baptist Union Corporation, had agreed in 1963 to release a strip of land known as 14-30, Hackney Road in front of the planned new church building. The frontage of 0.229 acres was exchanged for 0.161 acres on the north side of the church, apparently to meet larger Council plans, including road widening. For fairness, the church received in addition £1800. The road widening never took place.[6] Ultimately the whole of Hackney Road and some buildings behind, including the Lecture Hall, became part of a conservation area.[7]

The contested land with Girls Brigade group and Harry Weston c.1965

The undeveloped Hackney Road frontage, so obviously useful to the church, became a major battleground between interested parties. Developers wanted to get this valuable site. One proposal involved building a factory. John Grooms were interested, along with other housing associations.[8] The church was determined to buy it back from Bethnal Green Council and made several attempts to do so.[9] The Council was going to sell to the highest bidder. The church, with the

Mildmay Hospital, made offers in 1990 of £10,000 and then £25,000. The more realistic price turned out to be much more. Rumour and misinformation about what was being done in secret deals can be traced through the church records for 20 years.

In the end, by a sudden move in1993 and having gained promise of funding, the Mildmay Hospital, long-time partner of the church, bought the frontage for £175,000.[10] There were very good reasons for this move from the hospital point of view, but the church was surprised to be so wrong-footed. However, this part of the story relates to the larger longer term development that leads directly to a new hospital and now to a brand new Shoreditch Tabernacle church. After all this, as we shall see, the church eventually and painfully won the right to retain frontage which gives access for the church to Hackney Road.

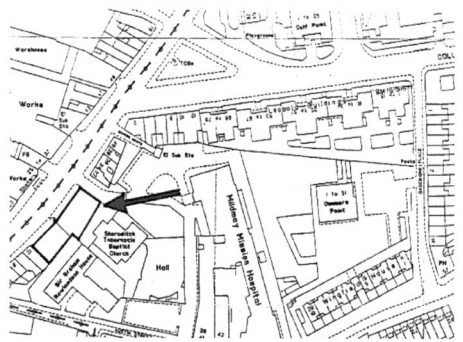

The Borough offers the contested land.

So much for a quarter acre strip of land. The second issue that occupied the church for the next 30 years was what to do about the Lecture Hall and how to co-operate with the Mildmay Hospital in their plans for needed development. It was decided by most observers that the Lecture Hall building had outstayed its usefulness. Year on year it cost the church substantial sums to repair and maintain. Ideas had been discussed from 1969 onwards that the Mildmay Hospital might have part or all of the Lecture Hall and its site, for a nurses' home, or for other building purposes.

In 1988 the Hospital was rescued from complete closure and the new hospital trust was eager and ready for change and development. The church (at various times) was willing to let the hospital buy the Lecture Hall buildings in exchange for land to compensate. The idea was to sell the Lecture Hall to the Mildmay Hospital and use the money raised to buy the Hackney Road frontage from Bethnal Green Borough Council and build a new church and hall on the remaining site. Over at least 20 years, land prices, surveys, building estimates, offers, refusals and negotiations follow each other in bewildering succession in the records. Nothing was ever finally agreed between the parties. In the end, perhaps in desperation, the Mildmay Hospital bought the frontage land from the Borough in 1993.[11] The church was surrounded, but not submerged.

While all this apparently unproductive effort was going on in the background the church pressed on with its work and ministry. Paul Henstock and his wife Lynda had left in 1988. Happily, the Rev Peter Clarke had come to be Chaplain for the Mildmay Hospital. Peter and Dulcie lived in a hospital flat next to the church and they became members of the church.[12] The church asked him to be moderator.

Peter Clarke

Initiatives in this period were both pastoral and missional. The seven deacons each took a list of members for whom to care pastorally.[13] Clarke also took time to do pastoral visiting and found many people still in dire poverty in the area.[14] A regular church newsletter was started to be called *Tabs*, replacing the previous *Messenger* and edited at first by Kath Mills, then a deacon.[15] A group of seven people were baptised in June 1989, two of them Anglicans.[16] A number of members and leaders participated in Billy Graham's *Mission 89* in June and fourteen referrals to Shoreditch were followed up in a Discovery Group and by the Mission Committee.[17] Not everything was well, however; a 'serious rat infestation' in the buildings accompanied these blessings.[18]

Naturally, the search for a new pastor began. Mike Nicholls from Spurgeon's presented persuasively to the deacons the idea of a student pastor from the 'Congregational-based Training Scheme'. It was resisted and quickly dismissed by the church.[19] They wanted a full-time minister. Baptist Home Mission visitors agreed the church could apply for a 50% grant. So Douglas McBain, then London Superintendent, gave the name of Hugh Doyle, MA, MSc, BA. Already a psychology graduate, he was completing his ministerial training at Regent's Park College. He preached with a view on 14th January, 1990. The members called him and he accepted. The induction on 15th September was a 'very happy occasion'.[20] He worked his required three probationary years at Shoreditch.

There was immediate progress in some matters. After years of unease and discussion, the 10.30 morning communion service was finally moved into the main 11.00 o'clock service.[21] An effort to reach the locality was actioned by the printing of 1000 cards which the congregation distributed round local homes. Financially the church was stable, under the wise hand of treasurer Daisy Berry. A 'nil grant' was made by Home Mission; that is, agreed in principle, but not transferred since it was not needed. Interest free loans from members and gifts, one of £1000, also helped the church.[22] However, at the end of the first three months Weston reported on the 'pastoral and physical benefits of the ministerial settlement'. Membership had risen to 67.[23] A controversial aspect of Doyle's mission agenda was contact with Browns, a strip club that still exists on the opposite side of Hackney Road. The owners were renting a church parking space, which itself was frowned on by some. But Doyle visiting the club and getting to know the dancers was a step too far for a number in the church.

A significant new venture began for the church in February 1991. Kath Mills and Violet Julier had been inspired by a pensioners' coffee meeting at nearby Victoria Park Baptist church and, together with other women in the congregation, started 'Contact Point'. It was a Monday afternoon coffee meeting in the Richard Pearson Hall for friendship and witness. They soon announced a successful opening and growing numbers. After a year they began to serve lunch as well and in 1993, for lack of space, moved into the Lecture Hall.[24] This successful venture continues in a different form today, although on Thursdays and Fridays. One of the older men to whom Beryl Rhoden served lunch was a local boy who tormented her small children in the 1960s.

Hugh Doyle was of the view that as minister he should be living within the immediate area of the church. The manse in Leytonstone was seven miles away. The manse was put on the market and Jill and Hugh Doyle looked for a suitable house nearer the church. The feeling that the minster and leadership were of a different background to the majority of members had been an underlying problem in the church since the very beginning. Doyle's instinct in wanting to move near the church was a helpful response. Prolonged negotiations and the search for a suitable manse went on almost until the end of his three years at Shoreditch. Unhappily he was not able to fulfil this wish.[25]

He gave his resignation to the church in July 1993 having accepted a call to Higham's Park Baptist Church. He expressed 'pleasure as a result of his experiences as minister at the Tabernacle' although his resignation was 'a surprise and disappointment' to the church.[26] Almost as soon as he had moved on, the house in Forest Drive East was sold and a town house was bought: 63, Chambord Street. It was only five minutes' walk from the church.[27]

Peter Clarke agreed to take up the role of moderator again and the search for a new pastor began. In June 1995 Peter Robinson BTh preached at the Tabernacle for the first time. The members were happy and called him unanimously at a special Church Meeting on 9th August with 25 members present. Robinson and his wife Carole were from New Zealand. He had trained at the New Zealand Baptist Theological College. He began with an eye for pastoral work and early on determined to visit all the members at home. The manse was to be used for discipleship meetings and for contacts from the neighbourhood and so it was agreed that a conservatory would be built. The annual report for the year noted five baptisms and 'signs of growth'.[28]

Peter Robinson

Robinson pastored the church for four years, the first three as a Baptist probationary minster. In this short ministry he stirred the church to think afresh about the needs of the local community. The Mildmay Hospital plans to buy the Lecture Hall and for the church to be rebuilt were on hold. Robinson, at a significant members meeting, pointed to the possibility of substantial funding, both from government sources and from the European Union. However, grants from secular sources would only be available on the basis of the church 'helping the community'.

These very important insights were to have consequences down to the present. Advice and promises of assistance came from the Hoxton Trust. It was also noted that any plan to demolish the Lecture Hall might result in a preservation order. The vision of the church began to shift from demolition to restoration. The building was surveyed and the architect said it was 'not beyond repair'.[29] The future began to look very different.

However, by all accounts and for whatever reasons, this was not a happy time for the church. Robinson was his own man, a visionary who 'thought in big categories' and had an instinct for significant change. He tried to change the traditional style of Sunday worship. But relationships were clearly difficult. At a specially called deacons' meeting, David Weston read a statement indicating he would not stand again as Church Secretary, he therefore resigned in January 1996 with regret. He was 'thanked for 26 years of faithful and dedicated service' as secretary and deacon. Baptised by his father in 1951 he was devoted to the Tabernacle, a deeply committed and influential leader in many aspects of church life. He had led youth work at significant times, played the organ regularly for services and had been Captain of the Boys' Brigade in its later years.

As a deacon and church secretary he served the church which he greatly loved through times of significant challenge and change. But the 250 member church he knew under his father's ministry in the 1950s was drastically altered. The numerous Tabernacle organisations serving the community had reduced, membership had declined and leaders were increasingly overstretched. The minutes record that there was 'continual confrontation' between him and Robinson.[30] Daisy Berry who had served with such care in the finances also resigned as treasurer in January 1997. She tried hard to work with Robinson, but could not cope with his plans to spend money the church did not have. Kath Mills became secretary and Sam Tunde became treasurer.

The newly shaped leadership encouraged the members to look forward and a decision was made in March 1997 not to sell or pull down, but to restore the 1890 Lecture Hall block; a shift in direction that was to have long and exciting consequences. Relationship difficulties continued however and Robinson was clearly feeling unsettled and unsure of his position. At the members meeting in July 1998 he called for a vote of confidence. The seventeen members present gave this, although they also noted that 'a Church Conference is needed to thrash out differences'.[31]

The vision of the church to use the Lecture Hall to serve people in need in the community was given impetus by the arrival of Mark and Bella Stephens who joined the church in February 1998. Within six months Mark Stephens became a deacon, along with other new members. This needed a hasty change of the church rules, though some wise heads strongly opposed such a move.[32] The church then agreed that the Stephens could use the building as a Day Centre for the homeless and vulnerable on a Saturday evening. It was to be called GEMS and within a few weeks there were a 'frightening' number attending which was 'putting the Tab on the map'.[33]

The church was still surrounded by large numbers of people needing companionship, support, food and advice as well as spiritual ministry. Between 70 and 93 people were being fed each Saturday.[34] In spite of apparent success in meeting these needs, within a year the relationship of the church leaders with the Stephens had broken down entirely. At a members' meeting in June 1999 an item raised by Bella Stephens, under the deadly heading of 'any other business', led to heated debate over kitchen cupboards. Robinson took everyone to the kitchen 'to sort the matter in love'. Sadly, the squall was the sign of a greater storm to come.

Evidence came to light of a private bank account, not monitored by the church or treasurer. There was loose accounting for money granted by the Church Urban Fund. Sam Tunde the treasurer was very unhappy. Bella Stephens was of the view that she was a 'Minister' appointed by God and was not answerable to the church or the deacons. Robinson and his leaders were very troubled. The matter was never resolved. The Stephens were removed from all offices and their ministry in the GEMS project came to an abrupt end, as did their membership of the church.[35]

However, the impetus gathered from this nobly motivated effort was to continue. The church made a new start with the work, renamed 'Tab People'. Early in 2000 it was consuming much energy, but was evidently valuable. Led by Ann James with a team of volunteers, it continued each week to offer 30 people 'a nourishing meal in a warm friendly environment'. She summed up the feelings of the church:

> God has given us everything we need to succeed... a wonderful opportunity to reach out to so many people and we haven't got to trudge the street either - he has actually brought them right here.[36]

Chapter 17

Courage for a New Beginning

The new millennium dawned and Peter Robinson announced he was leaving. He had been called to Poverest Road Baptist Church in Petts Wood. Carole Robinson had been unwell for some time and was advised to move out of the city. They had moved early in 1999 from the terraced manse in Chambord Street to Bromley Common. Before long the nearby church had invited him to the pastorate and he served there until 2008.

Pat Took, the Metropolitan Regional Team Leader met the deacons to consult about the future. Colin Marchant, a widely experienced Baptist minister with many years ministry in East London, was also present and he was appointed moderator.[1] He would preach once a month, but the members immediately gathered themselves for a new challenge. Ian Hastings arranged for visiting preachers. For evening services William Ade-onojobi and Funmi Afuwape stepped up to preach, Ann James and Sam Tunde led worship.

The church membership was now 62 with 33 attending regularly. An analysis of the church showed the profile as:

Black	- 29,
Non-black	- 33
Female	- 40
Male	- 23
Under 12	- 14
Teenagers	- 6
Aged 20-50	- 29
Aged over 50	- 31

Contact Point was still running well, headed by Kath Mills and Violet Julier, with at least 30 attending each week. Tab People also had a large number, on one occasion serving a meal to over 76 people.[2]

In December 2000 on a wet night with rain dripping into buckets in the Richard Pearson Room, Sarah Parry BA, the minister of a Baptist church in Chorleywood came to meet with the moderator and deacons. It all began well. She found 'instant rapport' with those present, noting that they were 'faith-based' and full of courage. The deacons heard her speak of a 'sense of grace' and of the need for the minister of a church in Shoreditch 'to live here in order to minister with integrity'.[3] She visited the church again and over the weekend of 3-4th February preached with a view to the pastorate. The members called her 'unanimously and enthusiastically'.[4] The Baptist Home Mission was to grant £5,000 to sustain the ministry. She also became a director of the LBA and member of the Home Mission Grants Committee. Parry and her husband Michael, working as a management accountant in London, were able to buy their own house in Albion Square, a mile and a half from the church. The induction took place on 14th July.

Parry soon took a strong lead and presented her priorities, based on the church vision. Members who had served in preaching and leading worship were encouraged to continue. The needs of the children and young people were to be explored and a weekly evening group initiated. The pastoral needs of older or housebound members would not be forgotten.[5] She also served half a day a week on the Mildmay Hospital voluntary chaplain's team. The church began to move forward fast and Marchant, who had enjoyed his time as moderator, could 'see evidence of the Spirit moving us after a rough start'. The membership roll was revised and ten people who no longer attended were removed.[6]

Sarah Parry with Michael

The first major practical project was to put the faded grandeur of the Lecture Hall in order. It was in sorry state, a burden both financially and practically for many years. Initially some work on the halls was agreed, to test if a larger project was viable. The buildings were cluttered with old 'stuff'. One room was full of doors. In March 2004 'skip days' were arranged to take away the accumulated items of many years. This cleansing demonstrated the pain of such changes: some members were going to the skips and taking things out again.[7]

All this took an enormous amount of time and effort. A Thanksgiving Service on Palm Sunday, 4th April marked a moment of transition as the real work was to begin. Colin Marchant preached. A former pastor, Paul Henstock, and former organist Len Sayer, participated. Parry wrote,

> The people at 'The Tab' have long dreamt of the day when these buildings could be refurbished and in thankfulness to God we rejoice that the time HAS NOW COME![8]

The Lecture Hall floor was sanded for £5k with a grant. Arts for All and other small charities were still able to use the building at a reduced rate. Meanwhile larger fundraising began. Melanie Hall had been employed for two days a week to fundraise for six months for a fee of £10,000. She was soon followed by Hannah Roberts. At an important church meeting in July 2004 a decision was taken to apply for English Heritage Lottery funding.

The church appointed Matthew Lloyd as architect. But the day to day work was done by Clare Warnock, who worked unstintingly and generously on the whole project. Money was already available from the Church Urban Fund and application was also made to the London Baptist Property Board for a loan of £70,000. These amounts turned out to be greatly less that the £1.7 million needed to rescue and refurbish the Lecture Hall building.[9] It was regarded as within the St Leonard's Conservation area and was listed Grade II by English Heritage in June 2002, which led to lottery grants in the end totalling £704,000.[10]

Other substantial grants and gifts were obtained, among them:

>   The European Regional Development Fund - £400,000
>   Borough of Tower Hamlets Neighbourhood Renewal Scheme - £58,898.49
>   Spitalfields Market Community Trust - £5,000
>   Garfield Weston Foundation - £25,000
>   Rank Foundation - £3,000
>   The Mercers Company Trust - £10,000
>   Tufton Charitable Trust - £5,000
>   The Big Lottery Community Fund - £240,000[11]

The contractor, Harry Neal, began work in earnest on 23rd August, 2004.[12] Most rooms were out of use so meetings and organisations were suspended. Contact Point and Tab People were relocated to St Leonard's and the Sunday School and Arts for All were given space in the Mildmay hospital. After less than a year the builders had completed the work. The members unanimously agreed that the building would now be named 'The Tab Centre'.[13] Saturday, 10th September, 2005 saw the opening, with tours of the building, a ceremony at the entrance and a concluding Service of Thanksgiving. The 'sympathetic refurbishment' had transformed the building; 'strangely familiar and brand new all at the same time'.[14] It was an entirely new start in many ways. A job description had been agreed for a Hall Manager. The first in this vital role was Andrew Sanalitro, who began work in April, 2005.[15] Much of the ongoing funding for a number of the activities in the Tab Centre was gained by his energetic initiative in co-operation with a succession of paid fundraisers, Greg Benson, then Graham Collings and finally Sue Higham. He was baptised on Easter Day 2006 and became a member of the church. A management committee was to work with him consisting (in 2006) of Sarah Parry, Eurannie Afuwape, Louise Alexander, Freddy Hernandez, Violet Julier, Amanda Allchorn, Caroline Barlow, Irene Impey and Fiona Lawrence. Four of these were deacons of the church.[16]

Andrew Sanalitro

By October the Tab Centre was running well, seeking 'the well-being of the local community, to enrich lives and to work with the vulnerable in society.'[17] As well as the usual church youth and children's activities, Contact Point moved back again on Mondays, with a cooked lunch for the over sixties, as did Tab People, 9.30 to midday on Saturdays, with a meal for the 'homeless and housed'. There was also the Tab Film Club, a Women's Group and a new venture in co-operation with East Sutton Park prison, the Bridge Project, to support women prisoners in transition and their families. Three years later a further project with women ex-offenders, All4 Recruitment, was started under Emma Pettigrew.

The Tab Centre immediately began making a modest profit from the letting of spaces.[18] Within two years the rental income to the church was over £136,000.[19] Using the building on this basis were Hackney Drug Action Team, Age Well, Shape, Volunteer Reading Help, Dalston Youth Services and City University Nursing. Later users were a number of partner charities: Shaw Trust (disability support), Arts for All led by Caroline Barlow, Made of Money (debt advice), Door of Hope (for sex workers) Somalia Employment, Hackney Play Association and the Actors Touring Company. Hundreds of people began using the building on a weekly basis. Most of these projects were funded by substantial and continuing grants.

National recognition of this excellent outcome came from the Royal Institute of Chartered Surveyors when The Tab Centre was given the Community Benefit award (2006), coming first out of 57 entries in the category.[20]

The Baptist Union also took an interest in the achievement. A portrait of Beryl Rhoden, 'Shoreditch Tabernacle, London', featured on the front cover of the Baptist Union Annual Report for 2005. They also sent a film crew to make a DVD film of the work of the church to be shown at the Baptist Assembly in Brighton the following May.[21] In it the inspiring story of the Tab Centre is told well, under the title 'Small Churches can do big things.' Parry and her courageous people certainly had.[22]

The headline description of the church was 'a Christian church and a community centre'. But there was very soon concern about the relationship between the Tab Centre and Shoreditch Baptist Church. The necessary management and commercial programme to enable social care and produce needed income had to be balanced with the spiritual ministry of the church and its other activities. Some were concerned that control over the Tab Centre was 'slipping away'. This particular possibility was not resolved for a number of years. To help integrate the ministry a monthly midweek service was arranged, held in the Tab Centre in place of one Sunday evening service. It was an opportunity for free expression and creative spirituality. Subsequently called 'Spirit Level', it soon met every week.[23] Parry also organised a monthly young adults group and started the Emmaus discipleship course.

The leaders and minister had worked immensely hard for five years and it is not surprising that it had taken its toll. Concern was expressed about Parry not taking proper time off. The deacons noted also 'the lack of commitment and the seeming apathy in the church'.[24] Some key members had died, some had moved away. Kath Mills had been ill with Parkinson's disease for some time and was in a great deal of pain, eventually to die in 2004, mourned by the members and by George, who had been an immense practical strength to the church in its transition. Fiona Lawrence took up the task of Church Secretary. Sam Tunde had moved away and Freddy Hernandez became treasurer in 2004.

So the Tab Centre was up and running successfully. Church membership had been sustained through a number of additions, including Olivia Hockridge-Omonuwa, who soon became Church Secretary and served ably till she resigned 2011 after 'the traumatic death' of her husband.[25] The deacons and leaders, though tired, were able to sustain an ongoing programme of services, Sunday School, Bible study and prayer meetings as well as Tab People and Contact Point in the Tab Centre.

Olivia Hockridge-Omonuwa

One of Parry's initiatives was Journey in Prayer, a 'retreat experience' arranged in conjunction with other local churches. The church was open for a two week period and those participating were able to meet with appointed 'prayer guides'. Journey in Prayer drew a good number of interested people and was 'highly recommended' by those who participated. It was repeated for several years.[26] The secretary included mention of many activities of the church in her 2007 Report.

> We were pleased to work with Tower Hamlets Social Services with the award winning Service of Hope on Mother's Day for families who have given up children for adoption. At Easter we enjoyed our usual Maundy Thursday service, Walk of Witness on Good Friday and a celebration on Easter Day. Harvest celebrations included a breakfast before the service and an auction on the following Monday. The Christmas season included a Christingle service led by Sunday School, Carol Singing in Hoxton market with Larry the donkey from Hackney City Farm, services on Christmas Day and a Watchnight service on New Year's Eve.

However, even while this challenging project to create The Tab Centre was under way, an almost unimaginable larger scheme was starting. Complete redevelopment was in view for the whole of the 'main site'. This included the Mildmay Hospital, the church building and all the land surrounding the Tab Centre. Ideas which had been considered for 40 years were about to come to fruition. From the very start of her time as minister, Parry with her deacons had been looking at options for the rebuilding of the 1963 church.[27] In December 2001 Mildmay Hospital hoped for £2 million to sell the contested frontage land on Hackney Road.[28] Quite understandably they needed substantial sums to rebuild the Hospital, but no one was in a position to buy it for the Baptists. To fund a brand new church it was agreed that a building with three storeys of flats above was acceptable.[29] The new church would have a purpose-built sanctuary, or worship space, suitable for a conference and performance venue, a small kitchen and meeting rooms. The plans also included a 'large internal garden' with potential for wide use by the church and local community.[30]

After planning delays and some significant changes to the scheme, Parry and Fiona Lawrence signed the contracts for the development on 25th March 2007. The property developer, Genesis London Ltd., was sold some church land and for their part agreed to build a new Shoreditch Tabernacle as part of the larger scheme with the Mildmay Hospital and blocks of flats. To carry the project forward Parry had a small dedicated team including Kath Mills and Sam Tunde, with the architects Mathew Lloyd and Clare Warnock and the professionals from the developers. However, it was finally to take another ten years to gain agreement and to build.

Parry set in motion this enormous project, but never saw its start, let alone its end. Pinned up in her study to read every day were the following words which sum up the spirit of the church during this time of preparation.

> We cannot do everything, and there is a sense of liberation in realizing that.
> This enables us to do something, and to do it very well.
> It may be incomplete, but it is a beginning, a step along the way, an opportunity for the Lord's grace to enter and do the rest.
> We may never see the end results,
> but that is the difference between the master builder and the worker.
> We are workers, not master builders;
> ministers, not messiahs.
> We are prophets of a future not our own. Amen. [31]

Throughout the history of Shoreditch Tabernacle it was loyal and dedicated deacons, supporting the pastors, who sustained the church in its trials and successes. This time was no different. Fiona Lawrence worked as an administrator for St George-in-the-East Anglican church for twelve hours a week or more, but gave herself for three afternoons to work in finance and administration with Andrew Sanalitro at the Tab Centre. She was also secretary for Contact Point. Olivia Hockridge-Omonuwa, mother of a young son, had a full time job as a senior project worker for Hackney Council, teaching home-making and gardening to adults with learning difficulties. As the church secretary she was a key support for Sarah and the deacons in all church administration. Beryl Rhoden was deeply involved in Contact Point each Monday, preparing, cooking and serving the lunches. This was followed by Club activity till 4.00 p.m. She also assisted with the running of Tab People, not least cleaning the cooker each Friday. The other deacons at this time were Violet Julier, Funmi Afuwape-Mercury and James Amao. Michael Parry served as Treasurer.[32]

Sarah Parry resigned in September 2009 and ended her ministry with the Christmas Day service. She was prompted by both personal and strategic reasons. The challenging Genesis development was now firmly moving forward, largely through her determination and drive. Ten years of ministry with such major responsibilities, as well as ongoing normal pastoral and teaching duties of a minister, was time enough. This was a good moment to pass on the torch. More important, she and Michael had decided to adopt and Sarah was to become a mother. They adopted Layton and Evan in 2010.

The plan for the 'Main Site'.

Chapter 18

Transforming the Tab

The management relationship between the Tab Centre and Shoreditch Baptist Church now came to the top of the church agenda. Stephen Little of Essell Consultants Ltd, Bolton, had been appointed by the church in April 2009 to examine the question of governance and advise the church. He outlined some possible approaches, finally advising that the church should 'set up the Tab as a company' and seek for it separate charity status. The church had also applied for charity registration, granted on 15th October. The direction of travel was diverging; the separation of the Baptist church and the Tab Centre. When Sarah Parry left, Little became the line-manager for Sanalitro in the Tab Centre[33] and trustees were appointed consisting of James Amao, Olivia Hockridge-Omonuwa, Violet Julier and Beryl Rhoden, all of them church deacons, with Meic Phillips of Mildmay as treasurer.[34]

High profile and influential Patrons were then appointed for the Tab Centre: John Barber, a deputy Lieutenant of the City of London, David Wheeler, a director of an East End accountancy firm and Caroline Haines a respected educationalist and freeman of the City of London. Barber and Wheeler also soon became trustees. These influential people were from a different world than the members and leaders of Shoreditch Baptist Church. Continuing difficulty about the allocation of management responsibility, 'who runs what' can be discerned in the records. It was assumed that 'two new charities (Church and Tab Centre) will ensure a better future' and it was noted that 'the Baptist Church does not preach religion in the Tab'.[35]

The church began to look at prospective ministers. With advice from Pat Took, the London Baptist Regional Team Leader, a decision was taken to seek an accredited Baptist minister to lead the church. A moderator was appointed, Mark Janes, the minister of Memorial Baptist Church, Plaistow. At their meeting on 27th June 2010 the deacons shortlisted three possible pastors from the profiles presented. Georgina Stride, BD, a recent Spurgeon's College graduate and associate minister at Victoria Park Baptist Church in Bow was invited for interview. The deacons commented that Georgina 'talks a lot', but agreed that the discussion will be pursued.[36]

She came to Shoreditch to preach early in 2011 and at the following members meeting the church called her as pastor. Among other obviously needed qualities, the church was 'seeking a minister who likes cities like ours and likes living in them'.[37] There was no doubt that she fulfilled this requirement. Born of Greek Cypriot heritage and with 'a challenging upbringing' in East London, she was living with her husband Steve in a town house on Isle of Dogs. Both were deeply committed to the area. She had a strong conviction of God's call for this new ministry from a vision linked to the book of Joshua; the invitation of the church was 'a door of hope' for her and the church for the future.

Georgina and Steve Stride

Stride began active work immediately, even though her official start date was not until April. The matter of the relationship between the church and the Tab Centre needed to be resolved. She quickly came to the view that separation would be a mistake. She was supported in this plan by the London Baptist Association and Regional Minister David Shosanya, by Andrew Sanalitro and others in the leadership of the church. The new patrons and trustees were disconcerted and there were significant differences of opinion. These reflected other tensions, as shown in a recorded comment that leaders were to 'bring squabbles and quarrels to Georgina Stride if they cannot be resolved. There should be no longstanding feuds or grudges held, in the church'.[38] She was inducted on Saturday 2nd April. A week later it was agreed that the church and the Tab Centre would be 'one body'. Ultimate control would remain in the hands of the deacons and the Shoreditch Baptist Church members.[39] A new Tab Centre management committee was quickly appointed whose role was 'to support Sanalitro'. The work of the Tab Centre would eventually become a separate charity, but under the primary control of the church and its minister and deacons.[40]

A number of initiatives began at this time, as might be expected with a new minister and some newly elected deacons. Stride had been chair of the Tower Hamlets Street Pastors project set up under Ascension Trust, a volunteer care ministry to the weekend night life. The church agreed to support this work and some members entered the training course to become street pastors.[41] The minister also initiated the start of the Alpha courses in the church with help from St Paul's Shadwell and Tower Hamlets Community Church. These regularly repeated courses drew in some who were to make a significant contribution in the future.[42] A 'cosy corner' was created in the church with sofas and carpet to enable more personal times of contact and prayer. With the prospect of a new church building in mind, the pews were removed and soft chairs obtained.[43]

There were also significant changes to the style of Sunday services. With no regular musician available, the congregation had been for some years playing compact discs to support the singing. In the early months of 2011 the congregation was sometimes only 14. Steve Stride was competent to lead with guitar and he drew in other players for sung worship. He organized a 'music academy' with professional tutors to encourage and train others, especially young people. A data projector was bought for use in services. These changes brought about a major shift in the whole way that Sunday worship was set up, led and experienced.[44]

In addition to church members having to adjust to a new style of leadership, it not surprising that the changes introduced in such a short time caused great tension. A few concluded that calling Stride was a mistake. Letters of complaint were written, by deacons and others, to the Baptist Union and the London Baptist Association about her style of leadership and over particular changes and decisions.

One example was Contact Point, the weekly over 60s group that had been running effectively for 21 years with a committee made up from the founder leaders and members of the meeting. A difference of understanding grew over who should be leading the church and its organisations. Relationships broke down entirely and after much pain on both sides Contact Point closed and its members went elsewhere. In a long reply to the letters, officials of the London Baptist Association did not apportion any blame. They said, 'Having heard the opinions expressed, we acknowledge that there are issues here that are difficult to resolve' and concluded there were 'different interpretations of events around what had happened.'

However, they were generally impressed with what was developing more widely in the church, in particular growth in membership and in the Sunday congregation. They recorded that 'the great majority of the deacons felt that things were going well at the church. All acknowledged that there had been a lot of change and much of this was for the better.' While accepting that there had been 'many changes within a short space of time there was an overall sense that the church is moving forward in the right direction. We were encouraged that new people are joining the church.' And they summed up; 'we are confident in Georgina and the deacons and trust that having looked at all the matters raised the church can move on and grow'.[45] Contact Point was soon started again and continues to run on Tuesdays as 'Over 60s'.

Important changes of personnel were also taking place. Steve Bird, who had quite recently become a Christian through the Alpha course in Victoria Park, joined and became an invaluable and practical supporter. Dave and Louise Leak came to help lead the first Alpha course and joined the church in 2012. Dave added wide church experience to the leadership, later becoming church treasurer, and Louise took a role in Sunday School. Gareth Jones joined the church and was quickly co-opted onto the leadership, later to be appointed part-time assistant pastor. In June 2011 Andrew Sanalitro resigned as Tab Centre manager and Christina Pilkington was appointed. Olivia Hockridge-Omonuwa had resigned in April 2011 as secretary and deacon. Of this decision she indicated a number of factors, including 'the traumatic death' of her husband, her full time job, responsibility for her growing son and having 'to juggle church politics'.[46] Funmi Afuwape who had been in the church since 1966 served for three years and then in 2014 handed over to Jackie Fearon, also a long-standing member, having been in the church since the 1970s.

Beryl Rhoden (↙), daughter Lorna (↖), Funmi Afuwape (↗) and Gloria Daley.

In spite of the significant difficulties of the first eighteen months of Stride's ministry, at the end of 2012 the church was able to report that,

> continual arrival of new faces has added to our richness and we are noticeable for our diversity of people from different cultures and backgrounds brought together by our Christian faith. We hold firmly to the gospel message that Jesus came for all and we attempt to welcome all.

The Sunday services were enriched through the Worship Academy so that there were now 'five young people involved and active in worship almost every Sunday.' During the year the services had developed from a single leader for worship to ten people able to play an instrument or sing, with still more wanting to join in. A men's breakfast ministry had begun in partnership with other churches.[47] A further venture, Tab Create, aimed to work with the many young artists and other creative people in the Shoreditch area. About 100 people came to the opening Sunday. A Sunday evening service was soon started to complement this venture.[48]

The congregation began to grow steadily in numbers, but soon the building work began, with demolition all around the church. By the middle of 2013 the disruption was having a noticeable effect on the hiring of the Tab Centre as a venue, particularly for weddings, a major source of income.[49] The work in serving the community pressed on. The 2012 report shows that on Thursday and Friday mornings Tab People, with a meal for the homeless, had '100 men and women attending each week.' A new café was set up in partnership with City Gateway and the building firm Ardmore Construction for the workers on the site. A new Community Dance and Drama Club began on two evenings a week for 6-16 year old young people with a grant from 'Awards for All'.[50]

Finally the day came when the congregation had to move out of the church building to await its demolition. Stride summed up the feelings of the members at the end of 2013.

> It is an exciting time, as well as it being a sad one, as we say goodbye to our church building that has faithfully served us for over fifty years. It's been a place and a home for many over the years and it has seen many get baptized and married, as well as funerals. Our last service in October was a great opportunity to invite many friends back as we celebrated God's goodness to us, as we opened and closed the doors for the last time.[51]

A year later the demolition had not started, but the church continued to develop, meeting in the Tab Centre with increasing numbers. 'Healthy and smart' structures were planned to enable growth, as new staff were appointed and new leaders emerged.[52] However, Stride records that 2015 was 'one of the most difficult years of my time at the Tab'.

Demolition began at last, but there were frustrating delays in the building programme. The time needed and the detailed thinking required of leaders who had other jobs, or a church to manage and pastor, was very difficult. There was a battle for the church to retain the exclusive right of access to the garden in the centre of the buildings. All this had 'negative effects' on everyone involved. However, there was invaluable committed help from many beyond the church in the complex legal, financial and practical negotiations. In the 2015 annual report Stride names a number of them.

> God has provided us with the necessary professional support we have needed, and often this has been given on a *pro bono* basis. We want to give thanks to the companies that have supported us during this difficult and exciting time. I particularly want to mention Kim Sangster our project advisor who is part of CPC Project Services LLP, Also for William Fryzer, a Partner from Dechert LLP who has given us invaluable support, and for our Partners at the London Baptist Association. Sam Spenser, a multi-disciplinary artist was giving his time and talent on a *pro bono* basis. He worked on the metal cross that was on top of the old church for inclusion in the new and he designed a war memorial for the men lost during the two great wars.[53]

Demolition of the 1963 building in 2015

In the development of the church during this transition period considerable value was found in times away. An annual weekend conference for the whole church began, 'to build fellowship beyond Sundays' and these bound members together providing spiritual input. Fifty people attended in 2016 with input from David Shosanya, one of the London Regional Ministers. The young people of the church attended Soul Survivor, national five day conferences held in a number of venues, to enable the next generation of youth and young leaders 'to worship God, learn what it means to live for Jesus … …, pray for one another, and to have loads of fun!'[54] Through attending these events church life and unity developed as well as bringing growth in numbers and vision for the needs of the world.

Personal transformation for a number of people came through Celebrate Recovery, a Christ-centred Bible-based programme, including Sunday teaching and midweek group work, to help people deal with 'hurts, habits and hang-ups'.[55] Emphasis has been put in very recent time on all members being disciples and disciple-makers. It is worked out in a number of conversions and baptisms to the great joy and encouragement of the church.

The congregation at the 180th Anniversary, November 2015 in the Tab Centre

In the 180 years of Shoreditch Tabernacle Baptist Church the basic spiritual and material needs of the people of the area have not changed. A new charity 'Transform UK' represents the continuing response of the church, headed up by Eddie Stride, Gareth Jones, now part-time assistant pastor, and Dominy Roe. The level of poverty, housing need and health problems may be better than they were in 'The Old Nichol', but the church is still a stone's throw from great social need. The impressive 19th century Tab Centre and the new Tabernacle Church sit on the eastern edge of Weavers ward, Tower Hamlets.

In the 2015 annual report on the Tab Centre Pilkington noted:

Weavers ward is ranked the 19th most deprived ward in London according to the latest Index of Multiple Deprivation. Adjacent wards have similar or worse rankings. In Tower Hamlets overall, it is estimated that 44% of households are in income poverty. This is the highest rate of income poverty across all local authorities in England and Wales and double the national average (22 per cent). Child poverty rates and Pensioner poverty too is a significant problem. According to the 'Indices of Deprivation 2015', income deprivation affecting children and income deprivation affecting older people show that the area around the Tab Centre is rated as 2 for child poverty (1 being the most deprived) and rated 1 for pensioner poverty. Statistically therefore, we know that the majority of people accessing our programme of activities are living in circumstances of poverty and deprivation. This is backed up by our experience of running the Centre for over 25 years and anecdotal evidence and the monitoring information we have collected over that time.

Minister and trustees in 2017, left to right: James Amao, Eddie Stride, Louise Leak, Gareth Jones, Rev. Georgina Stride, Jackie Fearon, David Leak
[Above; Dr Edward Abimbola]

Equally important is the members' vision for the future. The Christ-centred mission of Shoreditch Tabernacle Baptist Church is clear:

> We believe the Church is the key to transformation in our community – and that by working closely with our amazing members, we can transform our society with the good news of

Jesus and the great values we hold to. We do this by our personal walk with Christ and by following Jesus' example.[56]

The 180 years of this significant church have been varied and full of trial. Very few of the people who feature in its history made a name for themselves. Few had any social or political power. They were ordinary and weak, often failing in faith or obedience. Many were desperately poor, both materially and socially. The yearning line of the nursery rhyme still resonates with many living nearby.

'When I grow rich, say the bells of Shoreditch'

Yet the story as a whole is astonishing. In this densely populated area of London, with its enormous social and spiritual need, a Baptist Church grew up and still prospers. Her people consist of thousands who loved, served and sacrificed in spite of times of decline and deeply damaging setbacks. Year after year, decade after decade, they regrouped, recovered and rebuilt, and made repeated impact for the gospel of Jesus Christ.

A Tabernacle is a place where God comes to live. It is where his reconciling grace is found. It is where his people meet and receive the power to love and to go on serving. That grace and power is the best explanation for the still continuing story of Shoreditch Tabernacle Baptist Church. The riches of its members, found only in Christ, are still multiplying. They are to be shared freely with everyone.

The 2017 Tabernacle looks out onto Hackney Road

Appendix 1

Ministers of Shoreditch Baptist Church

Charles Bathurst Woodman	*1832-33*	*Ebenezer Chapel, Mason's Court*
James Smith	1833-38	Cumberland Street then Providence Chapel
William Miall	1839-52	(to Queen's Road, Dalston until 1879)
Hugh Killen	*1843-47*	*Only at Cumberland Street*
Charles Smith	1852-55	(Cumberland Street 1848-52)
John Russell	1856-69	
William C. Jones	1869-71/2	
William Cuff	1872-1917	Providence Chapel, then Shoreditch Tabernacle
John Edmonds	*1913-15*	*Co-Pastor*
Daniel Hayes	1919-22	With Mrs Hayes and deaconesses
Alfred Butler	1923-28	
Ernest Clifford	1929-46	
Harry Weston	1947-64	
Gordon Giller	1967-72	
Paul Henstock Lynda Henstock	1978-89	Co-Pastors of Shoreditch and Dalston with Salters' Hall (Baxter Road)
Hugh Doyle	1990-93	
Peter Robinson	1992-2000	
Sarah Parry	2001-10	
Georgina Stride	2011- Present	

Appendix 2

Deaconesses of Shoreditch Baptist Church; 1919-1968

The Deaconesses appointed by the church served at Shoreditch and in the work at Queen's Road, Dalston (at Pownall Road after 1943). In the record they are all designated 'Sister', although some are not given their full names and some in the early period were not accredited as deaconesses, or trained. Some took new, professional first names, and some subsequently married and changed their second name as well, so their trail is difficult to follow. For example, Sister Jessie married a Shoreditch deacon and returned to the church in 1941 as Mrs A. Baynton. There seem to have been at least 26 over 50 years, some returning for a second term.

At Shoreditch Tabernacle	At Queen's Road
S. Laura (1919 - d. 1923)	
S. Rose (1920)	
S. Mabel (1920)	
S. Ivy (1921)	S. Mabel
May Lofts (1923-27) S. Margaret	Rose Hicks (1928-30) S. Rosa
Ruth Dyer (1924- ?) S. Ruth	
Mary E. Young (1925-29) S. Myrtle	
Bessie Hughes (1927-30) S. Bessie	Lorna Doone Ridd (1930-32) S. Lorna
Mary Davis (1929-34) S. Mary	
Bertha Beale (1930-35 and 1937) S. Bertha	
Mary Smith (1930) S. Mary	Miss Marjorie Owen (1935)
Katherine Tebbutt (1934-38) S. Jessie	S. Marguerite (1938)
Alice Clara Morris (1935-38) S. Pauline	
Dorothy Finch (1938-46) S. Dorothy	
Hilda Bromley (1938-39) S. Hilda (and Queens Road)	
Alice Redfern (1940- d.1942) S. Alice	S. Bertha (1941)
S. Violet (1941-43)	
Marjorie Lillian Howden (1944-50) S. Marjorie (and Pownall Road)	
Mary Williams (1946-49) S. Mary	
Daisy Joan McGill (1951-59) S. Joan (and Pownall Road)	
(Winifred Willmott assists in 1958. S. Winifred)	
Elsie Drewett (1959-68) S. Elsie	

Acknowledgements

Most of the research for this book was done though searching the archives of Shoreditch Baptist Church, but many individuals have contributed. Encouragement and ideas about the project came from my Spurgeon's colleagues, Peter Morden, Ian Randall and Pieter Lalleman. Mike Elston assisted in proof reading. Significant material came from present and past members as well as others with long memories. Among these are: Keith and Joan Sobey, Violiet Julier, Beryl Rhoden, Terry Jellis, Ted Hale, Faith Bowers, Funmi Apuwafe, Jackie Fearon, and Gloria Daley. Further insights came from previous church staff and their spouses and from student ministers: David and Jane Brownnutt, Derek Allan, and Peter and Dulcie Clarke. Elsie Drewett, the last deaconess of the church, now 93, provided an entertaining and informative range of comment. Her nephew, Leslie Easton, offered valuable photographs. The previous and present ministers, Sarah Parry and Georgina Stride, gave important guidance about the last 20 years.

John and Lesleyanne Woolvett have generously provided vital detail about the Perkins and Woolvett family history, tracing the origins and long family involvement with the church.

Thanks also are due to Susan Tredinnick, chief cook for the Tab People, who went with enthusiasm on a number of expeditions to various places checking detail. She also created a large file of detailed research material on men of the Great War. Ann Buxton and Juliana French helped to source material and recent photos.

A tribute also needs to be paid to David Evans for his accurate and insightful writing in the previous history of the church, as well as his large and invaluable collection of notes. This work was an essential guide in setting out the story up to 1985. The task for the later years was more difficult without it.

Thanks are due also to the Baptist Historical Society and their secretary Steven Copson, for agreeing to publication with the co-operation of Adam Granger from AlphaGraphics North East who gave careful advice about the printing process.

Bibliography

Most of the primary source references are from the minute books, records, magazines and publications of Providence Chapel, Shoreditch and Shoreditch Tabernacle Baptist Church, its associated institutions and missions. These are presently held at Shoreditch Baptist Church.

1. Primary Sources

a. Journals and Newspapers

Baptist Magazine and Literary Review

Baptist Times

Chemical News and Journal of Industrial Science

Herald (Scotland)

Illustrated London News

Journals of the House of Lords

London Gazette.

New Zealand Herald

Press (NZ)

Psypioneer

Primitive Church Magazine

Shoreditch Observer

The Spectator

The Spiritual Magazine or, Saint's Treasury

The Sword and Trowel

The Times

b. Books, pamphlets and manuscripts

A Handbook to the Places of Public Worship in London (New Edition) with a List of the Clergymen and Ministers and Reference to the Places at which they Officiate, (London: Sampson Lowe, 1851)

A Travelling Correspondent [G. Holden Pike] *The Rev William Cuff in Shoreditch: realistic sketches of East London life and work*, with *The Holy War in Shoreditch* (London: James Clarke, 1878)

Booth, Charles, *Life and Labour of the People in London, Third series, Religious Influences Vol 2, London North of the Thames, The Inner Ring* (London, 1902)

Cole, Emily, *Report on Shoreditch Tabernacle Church Hall 18-20 Hackney Road E2* (Historical Analysis and Research Team, Tower Hamlets Borough Council, 2000)

Crisp, James, *Mrs Elliston's MSS.*, 1923; Shoreditch Tabernacle archives.

Cuff, William, *Fifty Years' Ministry, 1865-1915: Memories and Musings* (London: Baptist Union Publication Department, 1915)

Cuff, William, *Sunny Memories of Australasia: places I saw and people I met, with a postscript titled The Holy war in Shoreditch*, by G. Holden Pike (London: James Clarke, 1904)

Lockie, J., *Lockie's Topography of London: Giving a Concise Local Description of, and Accurate etc.* (London: 1810)

London Borough of Tower Hamlets, *Hackney Road Conservation Area Guide,* (2009) and London Borough of Hackney, *Hackney Road Conservation Area Appraisal,* (2009)

Mildmay Mission Hospital, *Minutes of Council,* and *Executive Committee Books*.

Parish of St Leonard's Shoreditch, Fifth Annual Report for year ending 25th March 1860 (London: Roberts, 1861)

Shoreditch Baptist Church Handbook and Souvenir, *Ye Christmas Fayr,* (Dec 1933)

Shoreditch Tabernacle Magazine, W. Cuff (ed.),(London:1878, 1879 and 1880).

Shoreditch Tabernacle Annual Report booklets, *Our Utmost for His Highest* (1934), *Shoreditch Calling,* (1935), *In the Midst,* (1937), *Inasmuch as ye did it unto Me* (1938) *A Good Investment,* (1946) *Workers Together with Him* (1948) *Christ's Commission – to preach, to teach, to heal* (1951) and 2005-2008

Shoreditch Tabernacle (1945) pamphlet LP 1792, 226.2 held at Tower Hamlets Local History Library.

Shoreditch Tabernacle Sunday School Library Catalogue (London, C. W. Brabner, 1881)

Smith, James, *Remains of James Smith: Being Extracts from Letters and Sketches of Sermons,* George Pritchard (ed.), (London: George Wightman, 1840)

Spurgeon, C. H., *Autobiography. Vols.1 and 2: A Revised Edition, Originally Compiled by Susannah Spurgeon and Joseph Harrald,* ed. by Susannah Spurgeon and Joseph Harrald, Rev. edn. (Edinburgh: Banner of Truth Trust, 1973)

Spurgeon, Charles, *The Letters of Charles Haddon Spurgeon, collected and collated by his son* (London: Marshall Brothers, 1923)

Spurgeon's College, *The Big Book* [Student record]

The Baptist Board Minutes, Continued from VI, 113 (Summary of the more exceptional Minutes, 1830-1835)

The Baptist Handbook and *Baptist Union Directory*

The Religious Census of London reprinted from 'The British Weekly' (London: Hodder & Stoughton, 1888)

Tredinnik, Susan, *The Shoreditch Tabernacle: Men of the Great War 1914-1918*. File of records held in Shoreditch Baptist Church archives.

Walker, Henry, *East London: sketches of Christian work and witness* (London: Religious Tract Soc., 1896)

c. Interviews and letters

Rev. Derek Allan, Student Minister, 1975-76. Phone interview 25th July, 2016.

Rev. David Brownnutt, Pastoral Assistant and caretaker 1981-85, Phone interview June, 2016.

Rev. Peter (and Mrs Dulcie) Clarke, Moderator, 1988-90 and 1993-95. Interview 10th Nov., 2016.

Rev. Elsie Drewett; Deaconess, 1959-68. Interview 9th August, 2016.

Leslie Easton, nephew to Elsie Drewett. Interview 30th Sept., 2016.

Rev. Ted Hale, member and ordinand of the church. Phone interview June, 2016.

Terry Jellis, employee of 1963 demolition contractor. Interview 5th July, 2016.

Violet Julier, member and deacon from 1938. Interview 22nd July, 2015.

Rev. Sarah Parry, Minister, Shoreditch Baptist Church, 2002-2011. Interview 26th Sept., 2016

Beryl Rhoden, member and deacon from 1962. Interview 22nd July, 2015.

Rev. Keith (and Mrs Joan) Sobey, Student Minister, 1953-54. Phone interview March, 2016 and letters 15th March and 15th Sept., 2016.

John and Lesleyann Woolvett, family archives and letter Jan. 2017

2. Secondary Sources

Allen, James T., *The Man and his Wonderful Message; Being the Life Story of Charles Haddon Spurgeon* (London: A. Holness, [ND])

Baker, T., *A History of the County of Middlesex: Volume 11* (London: Victoria County History, 1998) p. 234.

Baptist Union Retreat Group Journal

Baptist Union, *A Baptist People Living the Life*, DVD (Didcot: BUGB, 2006)

Bowers, Brian, *In Trust and by Faith* (London Baptist Association, 2005)

Bowers, Faith, *A Bold Experiment: The Story of Bloomsbury Chapel and Bloomsbury Central Baptist Church, 1848-1999* (London: Bloomsbury Central Baptist Church, 1999)

Bowers, Faith, (2009) *Keeping the Home Fires Burning*, Baptist Quarterly, 43:2, pp. 77-96.

Bowers F., J. Kapolyo and I. Olofinjana, (eds.) *Encountering London, London Baptists in the 21st Century* (London Baptist Association, 2015)

Breed, G. R., *Calvinism and Communion in Victorian England: Studies in Nineteenth-Century Strict -Communion Baptist Ecclesiology: Comprising the Minutes of the London Association of Strict Baptist Ministers and Churches, 1846-1855 and the Ramsgate Chapel Case, 1862* (Springfield, Miss.: Particular Baptist P., 2008).

Briggs, John H.Y., *The English Baptists of the 19th Century*, A History of the English Baptists, Vol. 3 (Didcot: Baptist Historical Society, 1994)

Creighton, Charles, *A History of Epidemics in Britain* (Cambridge University Press, 1894)

Curl, J. S., *Victorian Churches* (London: Batsford/English Heritage, 1995)

Deweese, Charles, W., *Women Deacons and Deaconesses, 400 years of Baptist Service* (Macon: Mercer University Press, 2005)

Evans, David V., *More Light, More Power 150 years of Baptist Witness in Shoreditch* (Shoreditch Tabernacle, 1985)

Evans, David V., *The Free Churches of the Shoreditch Area of London 1870-1918*. Dissertation submitted for the Degree of B.A. (with Honours) in Theology (C.N.A.A.) (Spurgeon's College, London, 1987)

Harrison, F. M. W., *"Go East, Young Man": An Autobiography*, (Private publication, 1993)

Johnson, W. Charles, *Encounter in London: The story of the London Baptist Association 1865-1965* (London: Carey Kingsgate Press, 1965)

Kibor, Jacob Z., 'The Growth of the Africa Inland Mission and African Inland Church in Marakwet, Kenya' in *Africa Journal of Evangelical Theology*, 24.2.2005, pp 107-128.

Maitland, S. R., *The Voluntary System*, 2nd edition (London: J. G. and F. Rivington, 1837)

McKenney, Helen G. *A City Road Diary 1885-1888* (eds. Alfred Binney and John A. Vickers) (Bognor Regis: World Methodist Historical Society, 1978)

Pook, Margaret, *The Leysian Mission 1886-1986, a century of caring* (The Methodist Church, 1986)

Randall, Ian, *The English Baptists of the 20th Century*, A History of the English Baptists, Vol. 4 (Didcot: Baptist Historical Society, 2005)

Shipley, C.E., ed., *The Baptists of Yorkshire: Being the Centenary Memorial Volume of the Yorkshire Baptist Association* (Bradford: W. Byles, 1912)

Skeats, H.S. and C. S. Miall, *History of the Free Churches of England, 1688-1891* (London: Alexander and Shepheard, 1891)

Tibbutt, H. G., *Mill Street Baptist Church Bedford 1792-1963* (Mill St Baptist Church, 1964)

Whitley, W.T., *The Baptists of London* (London: Kingsgate P., [N.D.]) (1928)

Whitley, W.T., *A Baptist Bibliography*, Vol.1 (Georg Olms Verlag, 1984)

Woodward, Max, *One at London; The Story of Wesley's Chapel* (London: Friends of Wesley's Chapel, 1966)

Young, Dr W. B., 'The Marakwet for Christ', *Inland Africa*, July-Sept, 1944

Notes

Chapter 1 The Founders (1829 - 1838)

[1] *The Musical Observer*, July 1913. p. 189 gives about 1829 as the date when Bradley hired a warehouse in Curtain Road.
[2] Probably Charles James Bradley, listed as shoemaker of Shoreditch, living or working at 111 Shoreditch. (Will 30.6. 1842 National archives Kew PROB 11/1963/283)
[3] Cuff (ed.) *Shoreditch Tabernacle Magazine*, (1879) p. 241.
[4] Lockie, J., *Lockie's Topography of London: Giving a Concise Local Description of, and Accurate etc.* (London: 1810)
[5] Map Of London 1868, by Edward Weller, F.R.G.S. Revised And Corrected To The Present Time By John Dower, F.R.G.S.: http://london1868.com/weller32b.htm [Accessed 13.7.2015]
[6] Woodman was a well-off eccentric who was mentally ill towards the end of his life. He inherited some of the correspondence of Jonathan Swift, and published on that subject. At one time he was a minister in the Moravian church.
[7] *The Baptist Magazine*; Third Series, No 86, Vol. 7, 1832, p. 367.
[8] Dissenting Academies Online: http://dissacad.english.qmul.ac.uk/sample1.php?detail=people&personid=2964 [Accessed 13.7.2015]
[9] Wellington Place Strict Baptist Church. Whitley, *The Baptists of London*, (London: Kingsgate P., [N.D.]) (1928) p. 149.
[10] *The Baptist Board Minutes*, Continued from VI., 113; Summary of the more exceptional Minutes 1830-1835, in volume H. p. 67.
[11] Letters of Charlotte Mary Yonge: http://www.yongeletters.com/people?person=2322 [Accessed 13.7.2015]
[12] *The Baptist Magazine 1835*, Vol 27 (Vol, 10 third series) (London George Whightman 1835) p. 426.
[13] Assignment of Release, M4, held in Hackney Archives.
[14] Cuff (*Shoreditch Tabernacle Magazine*, 1879, p. 241) refers to it as 'Worship Street', where there was a large chapel, clearly marked on the 1872 Ordnance Survey map, formerly used by General Baptists and then other denominations. But the Chapel round the corner is where the Mason's Court congregation went, between 16 and 17 Cumberland Street on the south side, as on *Cruchley's New Plan Of London Improved*, 1827 and on Cross's New Plan Of London, 1850.
[15] *The Baptist Magazine for 1835*, (Volume 10, third series) (London: George Wightman, 1835) p. 426 and *Ordnance Survey* map, 1872.
[16] *The Baptist Magazine 1835*, Vol. 27 (Vol. 10 third series) (London: George Whightman, 1835), p. 426. The old church, 'Providence Chapel' was between 4 and 8 Austin Street. *Baptist Chapels in or near London, Supplement, 1848*, p.783.
[17] On Cooper's Gardens, south of the present Columbia Road. Rebuilt in 1853. *Minutes* March 31st. Public Record Office, C 54/13037, mm. 26-32. 'Sittings for 550', marked on Ordnance Survey map, 1872
[18] *Baptist Magazine and Literary Review*, Volume 28, J. Burditt and W. Button, 1836, p. 259.
[19] 'Sittings for 700'; Ordnance Survey map, 1872.
[20] *Remains of James Smith*, ed. George Pritchard, (London: George Wightman 1840) p.91. Letter, April, 3 1837.

[21] *Remains*, p. 85.
[22] *Remains*, p. 87.

Chapter 2 The Take-over (1839 - 1853)

[1] *The Baptist Magazine 1840*, Vol 32, (Vol. 3 fourth series) (London: George Wightman, 1840) p. 24.
[2] Whitley, *The Baptists of London*, p. 165. This accounts for Cuff's later error that there was a Cumberland Street church 'off Hackney Road' (*Magazine*, 1879, p. 242-3).
[3] This was a substantial chapel called variously: Providence Hall Finsbury, Union Chapel and Cumberland Street Chapel Shoreditch. The name of each church meeting there is also variously called after the name of the chapel when they hired it.
[4] Assignment of Release, M4, held in Hackney Archives.
[5] Crisp, *MSS*, 1923.
[6] Whitley, W.T., *The Baptists of London* (London: Kingsgate P., [N.D.] 1928) p. 165.
[7] *The Baptist Magazine*, Vol. 34 (series 4, vol. 5) (London: Houlston & Stoneman, 1842) p. 26.
[8] *Minutes*, Feb 26th 1847 and March 24th 1848.
[9] Miall, W., *Can it be True? An Inquiry as to the Endlessness of Future Punishment*. (Elliot Stock, 1869) '[H]e presses the adherents of the popular doctrine very hard. A man who believes that nine-tenths of mankind will go into endless torments must be a madman if he begets children, and inconceivably hard of heart if he can enjoy a single hour of peace.' Review in *The Spectator*, 9th Jan 1869, p. 24.
[10] *Minutes* October 28th 1852.
[11] Free Christian Union, *Minute Book*, pp.105 – 7; F.C.U., 24.132(17) and James Drummond *The Life and Letters of James Martineau*, Vol. 1(BiblioBazaar, 2008) p. 435.
[12] *Psypioneer*, Ed, Paul Gaunt, Vol. 2, No 8; August 2006, p.169 and Vol. 3, No 7; July 2007, p.150.
[13] *Minutes*, March 22nd 1844.
[14] *Minutes* Feb 24th 1843.
[15] *Minutes* May 31st 1844.
[16] *Minutes* 28th June, 26th July and October 25th 1844.
[17] *Minutes*, Aug 30th 1852.
[18] *Minutes* October 24th 1845.
[19] *Minutes* Jan 25th 1850.
[20] *Minutes* July 28th 1848.
[21] *Minutes* Nov. 26th 1849.
[22] *Minutes*, July 28th 1851.
[23] *Minutes*, July 9th 1852.
[24] *Minutes*, May 31st 1852.
[25] *Minutes*, June 7th 1852.
[26] Lewis, *Topographical Dictionary of England*. (1849), iv. 4.
[27] *Minutes*, August 30th 1852.
[28] *Minutes*, Sept 14th 1852.

Chapter 3 The Church Goes Back Home (1854 - 1871)

[1] *A handbook to the places of public worship in London, containing also an alphabetical list of all the clergymen and ministers and reference to the places at which they officiate* (London: Samson & Rowe, 1848) p. 77.

[2] *The Spiritual Magazine or, Saint's Treasury*, Vol. IX (London: E. Palmer, 1833) p. 147.
[3] Breed, G. R., *Calvinism and Communion in Victorian England* (Springfield, Miss.: Particular Baptist P., 2008) p. 61.
[4] *Primitive Church Magazine I*, New Series no.7, July 1844, p. 364.
[5] *Baptist Magazine and Literary Review*, Volume 40 (J. Burditt and W. Button, 1848) p. 558.
[6] *The Baptist Magazine for 1848*, Vol. XL (Series IV, Vol. XI) pp. 428 and 750.
[7] *A handbook to the places of public worship in London*, p. 77.
[8] Breed, *Calvinism*, p. 137.
[9] Breed, *Calvinism*, pp. 24 and 29.
[10] *Minutes* 14th Sept. 1852.
[11] *Minutes*, 3rd August 1854.
[12] Letter Tuesday, May 1855. Spurgeon, C. H., *Autobiography. Vol.1: the Early Years, 1834-1859: A Revised Edition, Originally Compiled by Susannah Spurgeon and Joseph Harrald*, ed. by Susannah Spurgeon and Joseph Harrald, Rev. edn. (Edinburgh: Banner of Truth Trust, 1973) p. 343.
[13] Letter of 23rd June 1855 in Spurgeon, C. H., *The Letters of Charles Haddon Spurgeon, collected and collated by his son* (London: Marshall Brothers, 1923) p. 71.
[14] Cuff, 'A Short History of our Church', *The Shoreditch Tabernacle Magazine*, 1879, (London: F. J. Robinson, 1879) p. 243.
[15] *Minutes*, 7th June 1855.
[16] *Minutes*, 9th August 1855.
[17] *Minutes*, 3rd Jan 1856.
[18] Letter attached to *Minutes*, Jan 23, 1856.
[19] *Minutes*, 24th Jan, 1856.
[20] Whitley, *The Baptists of London*, p. 165.
[21] Creighton, Charles, *A History of Epidemics in Britain* Vol 2, (CUP, 1894) p. 593.
[22] *Journals of the House of Lords*, Volume 82, H.M. Stationery Office, 1850, p. 269.
[23] *Minutes*, 22nd April, 1858.
[24] *The Baptist Magazine for 1835*, (Volume 10, third series) (London: George Wightman, 1835) p.426.
[25] *Minutes* April 20th 1842.
[26] Hackney Library Archives, ref. M4, 1841, Cumberland Street, Union Chapel.
[27] *London Evening Standard*, 13 Oct, 1859.
[28] *Parish of St Leonard's Shoreditch, Fifth Annual Report for year ending 25th March 1860* (London; Roberts, 1861). List of Vestrymen, p. 35, also 1859, p. 29.
[29] *Shoreditch Observer*, London, 11 Jan., 1862.
[30] *Minutes* 5th June 1856. Whitley calls him 'Johnson' Russell, *The Baptists*, p. 165.
[31] *Minutes*, 28th May 1856.
[32] Cuff, *Fifty Years'*, 1910, p. 35.
[33] Crisp, *Mrs Elliston's MSS.*, 1923. In Shoreditch church archives.
[34] *Magazine 1878*, p. 99.
[35] *Magazine, 1879*, p. 243.
[36] *Magazine 1878*, p. 99.
[37] *Magazine 1879*, pp. 247.
[38] Went to Trinity, Horton Lane, Bradford; *Magazine, 1879*, p. 246 and Brown Morgan, J. and C.E. Shipley, *The Baptists of Yorkshire*. http://www.genuki.org.uk/big/engYKS/Misc/BaptistChurches/WRY/BradfordTrinityHorton LaneBaptistChurch.html (Accessed 23.7.15)
[39] *Minutes*, 26th August, 1858.
[40] *Magazine*, 1879, p. 243.
[41] *New Zealand Herald*, Volume XVII, Issue 5908, 23 October 1880, p. 7.

[42] A Travelling Correspondent, *The Holy War In Shoreditch*, p. 147.

Chapter 4 William Cuff (1872 - 1879)

[1] Spurgeon, C. H., *Autobiography. Vol.2: the Full Harvest, 1860-1892: A Revised Edition, Originally Compiled by Susannah Spurgeon and Joseph Harrald*, ed. by Susannah Spurgeon and Joseph Harrald, Rev. edn. (Edinburgh: Banner of Truth Trust, 1973). pp. 93-94.
[2] A Travelling Correspondent, *The Rev William Cuff in Shoreditch: realistic sketches of East London life and work* (London: James Clarke, 1878) p.11.
[3] Spurgeon, C. H., *Autobiography. Vol.2*, p. 94.
[4] Spurgeon, Letter April 1855, *Autobiography, Vol. 1*, p. 343.
[5] *Magazine 1879*, p. 244.
[6] Cuff, W, *Fifty Years' Ministry, 1865-1915: Memories and Musings* (London: Baptist Union Publication Department, 1915) pp. 26-27.
[7] Cuff, *Fifty Years'*, p. 21.
[8] Cuff, *Fifty Years'*, p. 26.
[9] *Minutes*, 18th Sept., 1872.
[10] *Minutes*, 25th Sept., 1872.
[11] *Magazine 1879*, p. 244.
[12] Cuff, *Fifty Years'*, p. 11.
[13] One of the houses of the London Society for Promoting Christianity amongst the Jews, in Cambridge Heath.
[14] *Magazine 1879*, p. 27.
[15] Cuff, *Memories and Musings*, p. 30.
[16] Completed 1867; *Minutes*, 23 Oct., 1872.
[17] Chris Miele, Report for English Heritage in *A History of Hackney*, Ch. 4.
[18] *Magazine 1879*, p. 244.
[19] *Magazine 1879*, p. 245.
[20] *Minutes*, 26th May, 1873.
[21] *Minutes*, 1st Dec., 1873.
[22] *Minutes*, 28th Jan., 1874, misplaced after 2nd Feb.
[23] *Minutes*, 21st May, 1873.
[24] Cuff, *Fifty Years'*, p. 36.
[25] *Minutes*, 5th June, 1873.
[26] *Minutes*, 21st Feb., 1876. 'Shoreditch Tabernacle Circular', in *Sword and Trowel Vol 5*, 1877, pp. 413-14.
[27] *Minutes*, 1st Aug., 1878.
[28] Mrs R Rowntree Clifford, 'The Call of Inner London', *Baptist Times*, July 21, 1931.
[29] 'Shoreditch Tabernacle', *The Musical Observer*, July, 1813, p. 190
[30] Cuff in *Shoreditch*, p. 57.
[31] *Magazine 1878*, p. 99.
[32] *Sword & Trowel*, 1877, p. 413.
[33] *Sword & Trowel*, 1877, p. 167.
[34] Cuff, *Fifty Years*, p. 53.
[35] *Magazine 1878*, p. 2.
[36] *Magazine 1878*, p. 27.
[37] *Minutes*, 23rd October, 1876.
[38] *Minutes*, 28th May, 1877.
[39] *Magazine 1878*, p. 63.
[40] *Magazine 1878*, p. 39.
[41] *Magazine 1878*, p. 63.

[42] *Sword & Trowel*, 1877, p. 413.
[43] *The Echo*, October 2nd, 1877.
[44] Spurgeon, *The Letters*, p. 170.
[45] *Magazine 1878*, pp. 39 and 51.
[46] *Magazine 1878*, p. 50.
[47] *Minutes*, 6th Oct., 1878.
[48] *Minutes*, 29th Oct., 1878 and *Magazine 1878*, pp. 123 and 134.
[49] *Minutes*, 27th May and 23 October, 1879
[50] *Magazine 1878*, p. 110.
[51] *Minutes*, 20th Jan., 1879 and *Magazine 1879*, p. 28.
[52] *Magazine 1879*, p. 54.
[53] *The Building News*, Nov. 8th 1878, p. 492.
[54] *Magazine 1879*, p. 104.
[55] *Magazine 1879*, p. 102.
[56] *Magazine 1879*, p. 102.

Chapter 5 The New Tabernacle (1880 – 1884)

[57] Mrs R. Rowntree Clifford, 'The Call of Inner London', *The Baptist Times*, July 21, 1931.
[58] *Magazine 1879*, p. 265.
[59] *Magazine 1879*, p. 265.
[60] *Magazine 1879*, pp. 246-7.
[61] *Minutes*, dated record after 28th Oct., 1879.
[62] *Magazine 1880*, p. 149.
[63] *Magazine 1879*, pp. 268-71.
[64] October 1879. *Magazine*, p. 219.
[65] Cuff, William, *Fifty Years' Ministry, 1865-1915: Memories and Musings* (London: Baptist Union Publication Department, 1915) pp. 51-52.
[66] Evans, David V., *The Free Churches of the Shoreditch Area of London 1870-1918*. Dissertation submitted for the Degree of B.A. (with Honours) in Theology (C.N.A.A.) (Spurgeon's College, London, 1987) p. 50.
[67] *Magazine, 1878*, p. 2.
[68] *Minutes*, 20th March, 1877.
[69] *Minutes*, 24th May, 1880.
[70] *Minutes*, 16th July, 1880.
[71] *Minutes*, 26th July, 1880.
[72] *Minutes*, 28th Feb., 1881.
[73] Banks, *Letter* 30th Sept, 1886; church archives.
[74] *Minutes*, 28th Jan., 1884.
[75] *Minutes*, 31st Dec., 1883.
[76] *Minutes*, 3rd Dec., 1885.
[77] *Minutes*, 1st April 1874 and 31st Dec. 1883.
[78] *Minutes*, 30th April, 1888.

Chapter 6 A Spiritual Community with Dinners (1881 – 1896)

[1] Booth, Vol. 3, 1902, p. 123.
[2] See *Minutes*, 27th May, 1878.
[3] *Minutes*, 30th Dec., 1872.
[4] *Magazine 1878*, p. 51.
[5] *Magazine 1878*, p. 62.

[6] *Magazine 1879*, p. 123.
[7] *Magazine 1880*, pp. 80-81 and 130-31.
[8] E.g. 50 in June - October 1885 and 69 in Dec 1900.
[9] *Magazine 1879*, p. 196.
[10] Letter, Shoreditch Tabernacle, Sunday, Sept. 18, 10 a. m. in *The Sword and the Trowel, October, 1881*. p. 536.
[11] *Magazine 1879*, p. 269.
[12] *Magazine 1880*, p. 87.
[13] *Magazine 1880*, p. 17.
[14] *Magazine 1879*, p. 126.
[15] 'Obituary: The Rev. W. Cuff', *The Times*, 22 May, 1926, p. 8.
[16] 'A Baptist Minister on Tour', *The Press*, (NZ) Volume LX, Issue 11472, 3 January 1903, p. 4.
[17] *Minutes*, 27th May, 1879.
[18] *Magazine 1880*, p. 241.
[19] *Magazine 1879*, p. 272.
[20] *Magazine 1879*, p. 271.
[21] Cuff, *Fifty Years*, pp. 31-2.
[22] *The Chemical News and Journal of Industrial Science*: Volume 31, Issue 788, Feb 12th, 1875, p. 74.
[23] *Minutes*, 12th Jan., 1885.
[24] Cuff, *Fifty Years*, 1915, p. 54.
[25] Walker, *East London*, pp. 74-5.

Chapter 7 Children and the School Room (1890 – 1903)

[1] *Shoreditch*, 1879, p. 57.
[2] *The Building News* 1878, p. 492.
[3] Walker, *East London*, p. 75.
[4] *Baptist Handbook*, 1890.
[5] *Deacons' Minutes*, 20th April, 1891.
[6] *Deacons' Minutes*, 21st and 27th Feb. and 15th March and Minutes, 19th March, 1893.
[7] *Minutes*, 1st May, 1893.
[8] Letter May 1st, 1893 in Deacons Minute book.
[9] Walker, *East London*, p. 75.
[10] Walker, *East London*, p. 76.
[11] Baker, T., *A History of the County of Middlesex: Volume 11* (London: Victoria County History, 1998) p. 234.
[12] *Shap Street Minutes*, Jan., 1899 and 30th Jan., 1904.
[13] *Shap Street Minutes*, 6th Oct., 1904.
[14] *Shap Street Minutes*, 25th April, 1898.
[15] *Illustrated London News*, October, 1863.
[16] Cuff, *Fifty Years'*, p. 45.
[17] 'A Baptist Minister on Tour', *The Press*, [NZ] Vol. LX, 11472, 3rd Jan. 1903, p. 4.
[18] Briggs, J., *The English Baptists of the 19th Century*, (Didcot: Baptist Historical Society, 1994) p. 355.
[19] *The Advertiser* (Adelaide, SA) Friday 20 February 1903, p. 5.

Chapter 8 The Sweet Air of Hackney Road (1902 – 1917)

[1] Cuff, *Sunny Memories*, 1904, p. 127.

[2] Cuff, *Sunny Memories*, 1904, pp. 130 and 137.
[3] Cuff, *Sunny Memories*, 1904, pp. 136 and 132.
[4] Cuff, *Sunny Memories*, 1904, pp. 134-35.
[5] Baker, T., *A History*, Volume 11, pp. 228-40.
[6] Pike, *Holy War in Shoreditch*, as in *Sunny Memories*, p. 154.
[7] *Deacons' Minutes*, 6th Nov 1913 and *Minutes*, 5th Feb, 1914.
[8] Pike, *Holy War*, pp. 155-6.
[9] *Minutes*, 17th and Oct, 5th Dec., 1904 and Cuff letter, *Minutes*, 6th Feb., 1905.
[10] 'Shoreditch Tabernacle', *The Musical Observer*, July 1913, p. 190.
[11] *Minutes*, 1st Dec., 1873.
[12] *Deacons' Minutes*, 16th Jan., 1899.
[13] *Deacons' Minutes*, 23rd June, 1901.
[14] *Deacons' Minutes*, 10th Oct., 1910.
[15] *Deacons' Minutes*, 5th Dec., 1912 and 9th Jan., 1913.
[16] *Minutes*, 8th May, 1920.
[17] *Deacons' Minutes*, 5th Nov., 1914 and 15th Jan., 1915.
[18] *Deacons' Minutes*, 8th March, 1916.
[19] *Deacons' Minutes*, 19th July, 1922.
[20] Detached notes in *Minutes*, 24th Feb., 1924.
[21] *Deacons' Minutes*, 9th Feb., 1926 and 10th Dec., 1927.
[22] *Deacons' Minutes*, 21st May, 1900, 2nd April, 1906, 29th March, 1909, 7th Jan. and 7th Feb., 1915.
[23] *Minutes*, 9th May, 1910.
[24] Spurgeon's College, *The Big Book*, No 848.
[25] *Minutes*, 13th Aug., 1914.
[26] *Minutes*, 10th Dec., 1914.
[27] *Minutes*, 14th Dec., 1914.
[28] *Deacons' Minutes*, 3rd Dec., 1914 and 7th Jan., 1915.
[29] *Deacons' Minutes*, 11th Oct., and 8th Nov., 1916.

Chapter 9 Spirited Sisters (1918 – 1927)

[1] *Deacons' Minutes*, 5th October, 1916.
[2] Recorded in *Deacons' Minutes*, 26th July, 1917.
[3] Bowers, Faith, *A Bold Experiment: The Story of Bloomsbury Chapel and Bloomsbury Central Baptist Church, 1848-1999* (London: Bloomsbury Central Baptist Church, 1999), pp. 231-33.
[4] *Minutes*, 20th December, 1920.
[5] *Baptist Handbook*, 1932, p. 321.
[6] Koven, Seth, *The Match Girl and the Heiress* (Princeton University Press, 2015) pp. 176-77.
[7] Walker, *East London*, p. 121.
[8] *Deacons' Minutes*, 12th Sept., 1919 and 21st April, 1921.
[9] Walker, *East London*, p. 90.
[10] *Deacons' Minutes*, 13th Oct., 1891.
[11] Rose, Doris M., *Baptist Deaconesses* (London: Carey Kingsgate Press, 1954) pp. 30-31.
[12] Tredinnik, Susan, *The Shoreditch Tabernacle: Men of the Great War 1914-1918*. File of records held in Shoreditch Baptist Church archives.
[13] *Minutes*, 2nd June and *Deacons' Minutes*, 19th June, 1919.
[14] *Baptist Handbook*, 1921.
[15] *Deacons' Minutes*, 21st July, 1920 and *Committee Minutes*, July, 1921.

[16] *Baptist Handbook*, 1932, p. 321 and *Minutes*, 15th June 1922.
[17] *Deacons' Minutes*, 31st July, 2nd Sept., and 16th October, and *Minutes*, 3rd Dec., 1922 and 16th Oct., 1923.
[18] Letter, Friday 9th Feb., 1923 in *Minutes* 11th Jan., 1923.
[19] *Committee Minutes*, 10th Jan., 1923.
[20] *Deacons' Minutes*, 8th May, 1923.
[21] Evans, *More Light More Power* (Shoreditch Tabernacle Baptist Church, 1985) p. 11.
[22] *Minutes*, 17th May, 1923.
[23] *Committee Minutes*, 4th April, 1924.
[24] *Minutes*, 11th Feb., 1925.
[25] *Minutes*, 11th Feb., 1926.
[26] *Minutes*, 25th Sept., 17th Dec., 1924 and 17th Nov., 1925.
[27] *Deacons' Minutes*, 10th March, 1925.
[28] *Deacons' Minutes*, 8th May, 1923 and 15th March, 1928 and 10th Oct., 1933.
[29] *Deacons' Minutes*, 9th Dec., 1924.
[30] *Minutes*, 16th June, 1927.
[31] *Deacons' Minutes*, 13th April, 1926 and 11th Jan., 1927.
[32] *Minutes* 15th Dec., 1927.

Chapter 10 Repair and Recovery (1928 – 1939)

[1] *Deacons' Minutes*, 21st Sept, 1928.
[2] Mrs R. Rowntree Clifford, 'The Call of Inner London', *The Baptist Times*, July 21, 1931, p. 518 and Evans, *More Light*, p.12.
[3] Bowers, Faith, (2009) *Keeping the Home Fires Burning*, Baptist Quarterly, 43:2, pp. 77-96.
[4] Clifford, P. R., Obituary, *The Baptist Union Directory, 1973-74*, p. 285-6.
[5] *Deacons' Minutes*, 19th and 26th Nov., 1928 and 8th Jan. and 27th Feb., 1929.
[6] Clifford, E., *A Good Investment*, Annual Report booklet, 1946, p. 2.
[7] Letter of F. Harrison quoted in Bowers, p. 78.
[8] *Deacons' Minutes*, 4th April, 1931.
[9] *Deacons' Minutes*, 21st Jan., 1929.
[10] *Deacons' Minutes*, 13th May, 1930.
[11] *Minutes*, 4th March, 1929.
[12] Evans, *More Light*, p. 12.
[13] *Deacons' Minutes*, 12th May and *Minutes*, 25th June, 1931.
[14] Handbook and Souvenir, *Ye Christmas Fayr*, Dec., 1933.
[15] *Shoreditch Calling*, Annual Report Booklet, 1935, p. 8.
[16] *Minutes*, 14th May, 1936.
[17] Sister Pauline, *In the Midst*, Annual Report, 1937, p. 10.
[18] *Shoreditch Tabernacle* (1945) pamphlet LP 1792, 226.2 in the Collections at the Tower Hamlets Local History Library.
[19] *Deacons' Minutes*, 11th May and 17th Aug., 1926.
[20] *Deacons' Minutes*, 8th Sept., 1936 and 12th Jan., 1937.
[21] *In the Midst*, Annual Report Booklet, 1937, p.16.
[22] *Minutes*, 14th Feb., 1932.
[23] Handbook and Souvenir, *Ye Christmas Fayr*, Dec., 1933, inner cover.
[24] United Committee report *Deacons' Minutes*, 19th April, 1921 and 13th Nov., 1923.
[25] *Minutes*, 23rd July and 8th Dec., 1933.
[26] *Baptist Handbook*, 1934 and Deacons Minutes, 11th April 1933.
[27] *Deacons' Minutes*, 11th July, 1933.
[28] *Minutes*, 1st Nov., 1933.

[29] *In the Midst*, Annual Report Booklet, 1937, p. 3.
[30] Sister Jessie, *Shoreditch Calling*, Annual Report Booklet, 1935, pp. 11-12.
[31] Sister Pauline, *Shoreditch Calling*, Annual Report Booklet, 1935, pp. 15-16.
[32] Evans, *More Light*, p. 13. Interview with Beattie Ellett, 1985.
[33] Interview with Violet Julier, 2015.
[34] *Deacons' Minutes*, 13th Jan. and 14th March, 1942 and 5th Dec., 1944.
[35] *Deacons' Minutes*, 13th June, 1939.

Chapter 11 Bombed and Blessed (1940 – 1944)

[1] Harrison, F. M.W., *"Go East, Young Man": An Autobiography*, (Private publication, 1993, p. 17) The book covers just the year 1942 when he went to work in India.
[2] Evans, *More Light*, p. 14.
[3] *Minutes*, 19th April, 1941.
[4] *Deacons' Minutes*, 29th Dec., 1940.
[5] Interview with Violet Julier, 2015
[6] *Minutes*, 19th April and *Deacons' Minutes*, 10th June, 1941.
[7] Bowers, F., 'Keeping the Home Fires Burning', *Baptist Quarterly*, 43:2, (2009), p. 81.
[8] *Minutes*, 3rd May, 1941.
[9] *The 'Newsletter'*, No 1, Sept 1947, p. 2.
[10] *Christian Endeavour Bulletin*, Shoreditch Tabernacle, July 1943. Bowers, pp. 89-90.
[11] *The London Gazette*, 17th April, 1942, p. 1.
[12] Harrison, p. 13.
[13] Letters to Harrison, 23rd March, 1944 and 1st March, 1945, in Bowers, pp. 80 and 96.
[14] *Deacons' Minutes*, 13th May, 1941.
[15] *Minutes*, 18th April, 1940.
[16] Letter in Bowers, p. 82.
[17] *Minutes*, 27th Oct., 1940.
[18] *Deacons' Minutes*, 9th Sept., 1941 and 14th April, 1942.
[19] Letter in Bowers, p. 83.
[20] *Deacons' Minutes*, 7th Dec., 1943 and *Minutes*, 28th Oct., 1944.
[21] Interview with Beatie Ellett 1985, Evans, *More Light*, pp. 13-14.
[22] Evans, *More Light*, p. 14.
[23] Letter in Bowers, pp. 85 and 86.
[24] *Christian Endeavour Bulletin*, Shoreditch Tabernacle, Dec., 1943. Bowers, p. 86
[25] Letter to Harrison, 4th Sept., 1942 in Bowers (2009), p. 86.
[26] *Baptist Times*, 11th June, 1942, p. 293
[27] Randall, Ian, *The English Baptists*, pp. 234-5.
[28] *Minutes*, 25th May, 1942.
[29] Mildmay Mission Hospital; *Minutes of Council*, 19 Nov., 1941, and *Executive Committee Books*, 21st Jan. and 18th Feb., 1942.
[30] Kibor, Jacob Z. 'The Growth of the Africa Inland Mission and African Inland Church in Marakwet, Kenya' in *Africa Journal of Evangelical Theology*, 24.2.2005, pp. 110, 120 and 124. (pp. 107-128)
[31] Young, Dr. W. B., 'The Marakwet for Christ', *Inland Africa*, July-Sept., 1944, p. 38.
[32] Drysdale, Neil, *The Herald (Scotland)*, Obituary, 13th May, 2013.
[33] Letter in Bowers, p. 86

Chapter 12 Adjusting to a Changed Future (1944 – 1947)

[1] Evans, *More Light*, p. 15
[2] Evans, *More Light*, p. 15

[3] *Minutes*, 22ⁿᵈ Aug., 1944.
[4] Harrison, F. W., *A Good Investment*, Annual Report booklet, 1946, p. 12.
[5] *Baptist Times* Nov 9, 1944, p. 12 and *Deacons' Minutes*, 5ᵗʰ Dec., 1944.
[6] *Deacons' Minutes*, 15ᵗʰ June, 1937.
[7] *Deacons' Minutes*, 14ᵗʰ Feb., 1946.
[8] *Deacons' Minutes*, 13ᵗʰ March, 1945.
[9] *Deacons' Minutes*, 17ᵗʰ April, 1946 and *Minutes* 30ᵗʰ June, 1946.
[10] *Deacons' Minutes*, 20ᵗʰ May, 1947 and *Newsletter*, No. 2, Dec., 1947, p. 2.
[11] *Deacons' Minutes*, 8ᵗʰ Oct., and 5ᵗʰ Nov 1947.
[12] Clifford, P. R., Obituary, *The Baptist Handbook 1973-74*, pp. 285-86.
[13] *Minutes*, 16ᵗʰ Feb., 1947.
[14] *Deacons' Minutes*, 13ᵗʰ Nov., 1945.

Chapter 13 Sowing so as to Reap (1946 – 1960)

[1] *Deacons Minutes*, 6ᵗʰ April, 1947.
[2] *Minutes*, 3ʳᵈ May, 1947.
[3] *Deacons' Minutes*, 20ᵗʰ May, 1947.
[4] *Deacons' Minutes*, 17ᵗʰ June, 1947.
[5] *Minutes*, 25ᵗʰ Sept., 1947.
[6] *Deacons' Minutes*, 11ᵗʰ Nov., 1947.
[7] *Minutes*, 19ᵗʰ Feb., 1948.
[8] *Newsletter*, No. 2, Dec., 1947, p. 2 and No. 3, March 1948, p. 1.
[9] *Newsletter*, No. 1, Sept., 1947, p. 1.
[10] Evans, *More Light*, p. 16.
[11] *Deacons' Minutes*, 15ᵗʰ May, 1956.
[12] *Newsletter*, No. 1, Sept., 1947, p. 4.
[13] Evans, *More Light*, p. 16.
[14] *Deacons' Minutes*, 10ᵗʰ Feb., 1948.
[15] *Deacons' Minutes*, 13ᵗʰ April, 1948.
[16] Local Press cutting, c. 1930
[17] Evans, *The Free Churches* (1987) p. 13.
[18] Tribute in *Deacons' Minutes*, 29ᵗʰ Feb., 1943.
[19] Evans, *More Light*, p. 16.
[20] *Deacons' Minutes*, 9ᵗʰ March, 1948.
[21] *Deacons' Minutes*, 10ᵗʰ Jan., and *Minutes*, 18ᵗʰ Jan., 1950.
[22] *Deacons' Minutes*, 20ᵗʰ March, 1951.
[23] *Minutes*, 11ᵗʰ March, 1959.
[24] Interview with Keith Sobey, June, 2016.
[25] *Deacons' Minutes*, 9ᵗʰ Dec., 1958 and *Minutes*, 11ᵗʰ March, 1959.
[26] Conversation with the author 6ᵗʰ July, 2016.
[27] Sobey, Keith, letter to the author, 15ᵗʰ March, 2016.
[28] Weston, tribute in *Newsletter*, Feb., 1957 in *Minutes*, 27ᵗʰ March, 1957.
[29] *Deacons' Minutes*, 19ᵗʰ Oct., 1960 and *Minutes*, 24ᵗʰ Nov., 1960.
[30] 8ᵗʰ May, 1960. *Minutes* 12ᵗʰ April, 1960 and Faith Bowers, emails to the author, 22ⁿᵈ March, 2016.
[31] *Deacons' Minutes*, 16ᵗʰ Oct., *Minutes*, 25ᵗʰ Oct., 1951.
[32] *Deacons' Minutes*, 9ᵗʰ June 1953 and 9ᵗʰ Nov., 1954.
[33] www.eltbaptistchurch.org/about-us/our-history/ (Accessed 1.7. 2016)

[34] *Minutes*, 26th June and *Deacons' Minutes*, 30th July, 1958 and The National Pipe Organ Register (NPOR) V.2.14, www.npor.org.uk/NPORView.html?RI=N16606 (Accessed 1.7.2016)
[35] *Minutes*, 9th Feb., 1956.
[36] Parry, Sarah, email to the author 29th June, 2016.
[37] Evans, *More Light*, p. 17.
[38] Interview with the author 5th July, 2016.

Chapter 14 Loved for What Happened Inside (1961 – 1967)

[39] *Rebuilding Account*, 22.2.65 in *Minutes*, 27th Jan., 1965.
[40] *Minutes*, 17th July, 1957.
[41] *Minutes*, 23rd Jan., 1963.
[42] *Deacons' Minutes*, 18th May, 1963.
[43] *Deacons' Minutes*, 19th June, 1963.
[44] *Baptist Times*, Feb. 24th 1927 p 130.
[45] www.mperkins.co.uk (Accessed 13.1.2017) and family material from John and Lesleyanne Woolvett.
[46] Report of the Corporate Director of Development and Renewal, *Applications for planning permission and conservation area consent*, June 2010, PA/09/2323 and 2324, 6.12 and 8.22.
[47] *Minutes*, 27th Nov, 1963.
[48] *Deacons' Minutes*, 15th May, 16th Oct. and, *Minutes*, 30th October, 1963.
[49] *Deacons' Minutes*, 15th May, 1963.
[50] *Newsletter*, November, 1963.
[51] *Deacons' Minutes*, 20th Nov., 1963.
[52] Keith Sobey, letter to the author, September, 2016.
[53] *Deacons' Minutes*, 1st Jan., 1964, 8th Feb. and 7th March, 1968.
[54] *Rebuilding Account*, 22.2.1965 in *Minutes*.
[55] Randall, Ian, *The English Baptists*, pp. 248 and 294.
[56] Interview with Elsie Drewett, Aug., 2016 and *Baptist Union Handbook*, 1969 and 1975-76.
[57] *Deacons' Minutes*, 9th Nov., 1982.
[58] Interview with Elsie Drewett and *Women's Report*, 19th Jan. in *Minutes*, 23rd Jan., 1986.
[59] *Minutes*, 28th March, 1968.
[60] *Secretary's report*, in *Minutes*, 30th March, 1966.
[61] *Minutes*, 26th Jan., 1967.

Chapter 15 Social Change and Political Action (1968 – 1989)

[62] *Deacons' Minutes*, n.d. Nov., 1964.
[63] *Deacons' Minutes*, 16th Feb., 1967.
[64] Group Fellowship Council recommendation in *Minutes*, 25th March, 1971.
[65] *Minutes*, 25th May, 1972.
[66] Interview with Elsie Drewett and *Minutes*, 30th Nov., 1967.
[67] *Minutes*, 28th Sept., 1967.
[68] *Minutes*, 25th July, 1967.
[69] *Minutes*, 26th Jan. and 25th May, 1972.
[70] Evans, *More Light*, p. 18.
[71] *Deacons' Minutes*, 20th July and *Minutes*, 27th July, 1966.
[72] *Deacons' Minutes*, 31st March and 14th May, 1970.

[73] *Minutes*, 25th Nov., 1964.
[74] *Deacons' Minutes,* 10th Sept, 1970.
[75] *Minutes*, 28th Jan., 1971.
[76] *Minutes*, 22nd March and 25th May, 1972.
[77] £2000 in 1964, £1500 in 1967 and £5000 in 1973.
[78] Interview with Beryl Rhoden, July, 2015.
[79] *Minutes*, 26th Sept, 1970.
[80] Phone interview with Derek Allan, July, 2016.
[81] Secretary's annual report, *Minutes,* 1977.
[82] *Minutes,* 16th July, 1979.
[83] *Minutes*, 25th Jan. and 29th Nov. 1979 and 15th May 1980.
[84] *Deacons' Minutes*, 3rd July 1978 and 17th Jan. 1979 and 27 Nov. 1980.
[85] *Deacons' Minutes*,13th Oct., and 10th Nov., 1981 and 14th June, 1983 and *Minutes*, 25th March, 1982.
[86] Phone interview with David Brownnutt, August 2016.
[87] *Minutes*, 28th Jan., 1982.
[88] Interview with Peter and Dulcie Clarke, November, 2016 and David Brownnutt, August, 2016.
[89] Paul Henstock letters to David Evans, 11th Feb., 1985 and 17th Sept., 1986.
[90] Shoreditch Archives, loose sheet, approx. 1985.
[91] *Deacons' Minutes*, 8th Oct., 1984, 9th Nov., 1990 and 10th Jan., 1991.
[92] Interview with Derek Allan, July, 2016.
[93] *Deacons' Minutes*, 13th July, 1982 and 12th May, 1986 and *Minutes*, 26th Nov., 1981.
[94] *Deacons' Minutes*, 12th October, 1982 and 11th March, 1985.
[95] *Minutes*, 19th Sept., 1991.
[96] *Deacons' Minutes*, 1st Dec., 1984 and 11th Nov., 1985
[97] *Deacons' Minutes*, 9th Dec., 1985 and 10th Nov., 1986.
[98] 'A Tribute to Paul Henstock', *Baptist Union Retreat Group Journal*, Autumn, 2015.
[99] *Minutes*, 26th Jan., 1989.

Chapter 16 Land and Love in Action (1982 - 2000)

[1] *Deacons' Minutes*, 12th May, 1986.
[2] *Minutes*, 19th March, 1992.
[3] *Deacons' Minutes*, 4th June, 1992.
[4] *Deacons' Minutes*, 12th March, 1987 and 8th Sept., 1988.
[5] 'Associate Membership' paper, *Deacons' Minutes*, 7th Sept. and *Minutes*, 28th Sept., 1989.
[6] *Deacons' Minutes*, 13th Jan., 1986.
[7] London Borough of Tower Hamlets, *Hackney Road Conservation Area Guide*, Adopted 4th November 2009 and London Borough of Hackney, *Hackney Road Conservation Area Appraisal*, July, 2009.
[8] *Minutes*, 25th Jan., 1990.
[9] *Deacons' Minutes,* 9th Sept., 1985, 8th Sept., 1986, *Minutes*, 26th Nov., 1987 and 15th Jan., 1990.
[10] *Deacons' Minutes*, 4th Dec., 1991.
[11] *Deacons' Minutes*, 15th July, 1993.
[12] *Deacons' Minutes*, 6th Oct., 1988 and 4th May, 1989.
[13] *Deacons' Minutes*, 8th Dec., 1988.
[14] Interview with Peter and Dulcie Clarke, November, 2017.
[15] *Minutes*, 24th Nov., 1988.
[16] *Deacons' Minutes*, 25th May, 1988.

[17] *Deacons' Minutes,* 6th July, 1989.
[18] *Deacons' Minutes,* 9th March, 1989.
[19] *Deacons' Minutes,* 13th April and *Minutes,* 28th May, 1989.
[20] *Minutes,* 25th Jan., and *Deacons' Minutes,* 20th Sept., 1990.
[21] *Minutes,* 17th Jan., 1991.
[22] *Deacons' Minutes,* 24th July, 13th Dec., 1990.
[23] *Minutes,* 17th Jan., 1991.
[24] *Minutes,* 17th Jan., 1991, *Deacons' Minutes,* 4th Dec., 1991 and 3rd June, 1993.
[25] *Deacons' Minutes,* 10th Jan., 1991 and 12th Nov., 1992.
[26] *Deacons' Minutes,* 15 July and *Minutes,* 23rd Sept., 1993 and *Minutes,* 19th Jan., 1994.
[27] *Deacons' Minutes,* 9th March, 1994.
[28] *Minutes,* 17th Jan., 1996.
[29] *Minutes,* 20th March and 15th May, 1996.
[30] *Deacons' Minutes,* 11th Dec., 1996.
[31] *Minutes,* 17th June, 1988.
[32] *Minutes,* 25th Nov., 1998.
[33] *Minutes,* 15th April, 1998 and 24th Feb., 1999.
[34] Report by Robinson in *Minutes,* 24th Nov., 1999.
[35] *Minutes,* 15th Sept. and Nov., 1999.
[36] *Minutes,* 23rd Feb., 2000.

Chapter 17 Courage for a New Beginning (2000 - 2009)

[1] *Deacons' Minutes,* 14th June, 2000.
[2] *Deacons' Minutes,* 13th Sept and *Minutes,* 15th Nov., 2000.
[3] *Deacons' Minutes,* 12th Dec., 2000.
[4] *Minutes,* 17th Jan., and 11th Feb., 2001.
[5] *Minutes,* 18th July, 2001.
[6] *Minutes,* 21st March, 2001.
[7] Interview with Sarah Parry, September, 2016.
[8] *Thanksgiving Service [Order],* 4th April, 2005.
[9] *Deacons' Minutes,* 11th December, 2002.
[10] Record of meeting with Melanie Hall 13th June, 2001. *Deacons' Minutes,* 12th June, 2002, 9th June, 2004 and 9th Nov., 2005.
[11] *Annual Report 2005, The Tab Centre and Shoreditch Tabernacle Baptist Church* and *Deacons' Minutes,* 11th Dec., 2002 and *Treasurer's Report,* 31st Dec., 2003.
[12] *Deacons' Minutes,* 15th Sept., 2004.
[13] *Minutes,* 14th Nov, 2004.
[14] *The Tab Centre,* lettings leaflet and Sarah Parry, *Letter of Invitation,* 2nd June, 2005.
[15] *Deacons' Minutes,* 14th Jan., 2004 and *Minutes,* 13th March, 2005.
[16] *Annual Report 2006.*
[17] *Introducing the Tab Centre* [undated].
[18] *Deacons' Minutes,* 8th June, 2005.
[19] *Annual Accounts 2007.*
[20] *RICS Awards 2006 ceremony,* 20 October, 2006.
[21] *Minutes,* 22nd Jan., 2006.
[22] *A Baptist People Living the Life,* DVD (Didcot: BUGB, 2006)
[23] *Deacons' Minutes,* 18th Jan. and 15th Feb., and *Minutes,* 22nd Jan., 2006.
[24] *Deacons' Minutes,* 12th April, 2006, 10th Jan, 2007 and 15th Jan., 2008.
[25] Letter to *Deacons'* and Minister, 6th April 2011 in *Deacons' Minutes,* 10th April, 2011.
[26] *Annual Report 2007,* p.8 and Church Secretary's report, March, 2008.
[27] *Minutes,* 16th May, 2001.

[28] *Deacons' Minutes,* 5th Dec., 2001.
[29] *Minutes,* 10th Feb., 2002 and 25th July, 2004.
[30] *Annual Report 2008*, pp. 18-20.
[31] From a prayer by Bishop Ken Untener of Saginaw, Michigan 1979.
[32] Profiles of deacons in *Deacons' Minutes,* 19th Sept, 2007.

Chapter 18 Transforming the Tab (2010 – 2017)

[33] Charity Commission Letter 15th Oct., 2009 in *Deacons Minutes,* 13th Oct., 2009.
[34] *Minutes,* 22nd Nov., 2009.
[35] 'Tab Centre Progress Report 2010', pp. 2 and 8 in *Deacons Minutes,* 10th Feb., 2010.
[36] *Deacons Minutes,* 1st Aug. and 23rd Sept., 2010.
[37] 'The kind of minister we are seeking' in *Deacons Minutes,* 7th Nov., 2010.
[38] *Deacons Minutes,* 20th March, 2011.
[39] *Deacons Minutes,* 10th April, 2011.
[40] *Deacons Minutes,* 13th Nov., 2011.
[41] *Deacons Minutes,* 10th April, 2011.
[42] *Deacons Minutes,* 11th Sept., 2011.
[43] *Deacons Minutes,* 5th Feb., 2012.
[44] *Deacons Minutes,* 13th Nov., 2011 and 5th Feb., 2012.
[45] Letter from Geoff Andrews and Kumar Rajagopalan in *Deacons Minutes,* 10th Feb., 2013.
[46] Letter in *Minutes,* April, 2011.
[47] *Report of the Trustees,* Dec., 2012, pp. 3 and 4.
[48] *Deacons Minutes,* 22nd March, 2014.
[49] *Deacons Minutes,* 16th July, 2013.
[50] The Tab Centre, *Review of Activities and Achievements 2012*, pp 1-.2
[51] *Report of the trustees for year ended 31st December 2013*
[52] *Report of the trustees for year ended 31st December 2014*
[53] *Report of the trustees for year ended 31st December 2015*
[54] https://soulsurvivor.com/summer/ [Accessed 3.2.2017]
[55] www.celebraterecovery.co.uk
[56] *The Tab Church Mission Statement and Vision: Steps to health and growth.* (Draft) 1st Sept., 2014.

Index

Abney Park Cemetery, 25, 77
Ackland, George, 62
Ade-onojobi, William, 137
Afuwape, Eurannie, 126, 140
Afuwape, Funmi, 137, 143, 148
alcohol, 77, 85
Allan, Derek, 122, 126
Alpha course, 146, 148
Amao, James, 143, 145
Arts for All, 139, 140
Associate Member list, 130
Association of Strict Baptist Churches, 24
Austin Street, 9, 19, 20, 70, 80, 100
Baines, George architect, 55
Bangladeshi school, 129
Banks, Lewis architect, 34, 44
Baptist churches
   Bloomsbury, 70
   Broadmead Bristol, 56
   Bury St Edmunds, 28–30
   Cambray Place, Cheltenham, 28
   Clover Street, Chatham, 26
   Dalston and Salters' Hall, 119, 122, 123
   Downs, Clapton, 33, 43, 119
   East London Tabernacle, 38, 94, 100, 110
   Grimsby, 68
   Hampstead, 50, 57
   Higham's Park, 133
   Kings Cross, 71, 116, 119
   Mare Street, 100
   New River, 119
   Open Doors, 119
   Queen's Road, 17, 18, 100, 113
   Ridgemount, 28
   Victoria Park, 100, 133, 145, 148
   West Green, Tottenham., 68
Baptist Home Mission, 132
Baptist Lay-preachers' Association, 107
Baptist Times, 63, 96, 109
Baptist Union (BU), 60, 70, 72, 74, 79, 82, 97, 100, 101, 104, 118, 128, 130, 140, 147
Barlow, Caroline, 140
Barnardo, Dr. Thomas, 42
Batt, Bob, 89, 90
Benevolent Society, 15, 58
Berry, Daisy, 121, 123, 133, 135
Bethnal Green Borough, 107, 131
Billy Graham meetings, 105, 111, 132
Bird, Steve, 148
Black, Sir Cyril MP, 113, 115
Boggis, George, 33, 43, 45
bombing, 89, 90, 93, 98, 99
book depot, 36, 50, 67
Boulton, Thomas, 9
Boundary Estate, 59
Boys' Brigade, 76, 81, 82, 88, 90, 94, 105, 121, 123, 127, 129, 135
Bradley, James, 7, 8
Bridge Project, 140
Bridge, Oliver, 29, 32
Bristol Baptist College, 8, 108
Brock, William, 50
Brown, Archibald, 38

Brown, Raymond, 109
Brownnutt, David and Jane, 123, 124
Browns strip club, 133
Bryant, Henry, 116
Building Society, 49
Butler, Alfred, 67, 75–77
Calvinism, 8, 15, 19, 21, 26, 30, 31
Cartwright, G. B., 84, 87, 91, 109
Cartwright, George, 33, 45, 63, 77
Celebrate Recovery, 151
Central Church, 70
Central Committee, 70, 80, 100
Chapel Keeper, 22, 50, 67, 80
charismatic movement, 120
Charlesworth, Vernon J., 48
Cheesman, Carrie, 109, 111, 117, 123
children's work, 37, 42, 46, 53, 57, 58, 72, 83, 86, 95, 119, 118–25, 138, 140
choir, 39, 52, 66, 76, 105, 106, 127
Christian Endeavour, 83, 94
Christmas dinner, 49, 50, 95
Christmas Fair, 82
church garden, 142
Clarke, Peter, 132
Clifford, David, 90, 100
Clifford, Earnest, 79–87
Clifford, Paul Rowntree, 79
Clifford, Ruth, 79, 81, 83, 92, 99, 100, 101
closed membership, 19, 21, 46, 76
coal vouchers, 85
communion, 15, 20, 21, 23, 29, 30, 125, 126, 133,
communion tickets, 40

Community Benefit award, 140
Community Dance and Drama Club, 149
Contact Point, 133, 137, 140, 141, 143, 147, 148
Country Homes scheme, 58
Crisp, James C., 7, 13, 26, 113
Crowhurst, Divine Healing Mission, 115
Cuff, Marianne, 37, 38, 72, 75, 77
Cuff, William, 22, 28–69, 52, 77, 106, 113, 115
   Australasia, 49, 60, 62
   bereavements, 31, 38, 73, 75
   BU President, 60
   Bury St Edmunds, 28, 30
   butchering, 28, 49
   conversion and call, 28
   death and burial, 77
   LBA President, 60
   Ridgemount, 28
Cuff, William Harvey, 37
Cumberland Street, 8, 13, 16–22, 23, 24, 113
Curtain Road, 7, 8, 19, 24, 113, 114
cycling club, 73
Daley, Gloria, 121
Deaconesses, 71–74, 77, 79, 92, 104, 109
   S. Margaret (May Lofts), 75
   Sister Alice (Redfern), 89, 92
   Sister Bertha (Beale), 84, 92
   Sister Dorothy (Finch), 83, 92
   Sister Elsie (Drewett), 115–18
   Sister Hilda (Bromley), 83

Sister Jessie (Katherine Tebbutt/Mrs A. Baynton), 83, 155
Sister Laura, 71, 75
Sister Margaret (Lofts), 77
Sister Marjorie (Howden), 92, 99
Sister Marjorie (Owen), 83, 85
Sister Mary (Smith), 84
Sister Mary (Williams), 92
Sister Pauline (Alice Clara Morris), 83
Sister Ruth (Dyer), 75
Sister Violet, 92
Deaconesses Order, 72, 82, 117
deacons, 9, 17, 24, 43, 45, 75, 81, 83, 84, 87, 92, 132, 140, 143, 145
deceased wife law, 24
Dorcas Society, 36, 58
Dorset Estate, 110
Doyle, Hugh, 126, 132, 133
Ebenezer Chapel Shoreditch, 7, 8, 24
Edmonds, John, 68
Education Acts, 60
elders, 40, 44, 45, 46, 47, 50, 71, 72
Ellett, Beattie, 87, 92
Elven, Cornelius, 30
Emmaus course, 141
evacuation, 90
evangelism, 36, 39, 48, 94, 108, 119, 122, 127
Evans, David V., 43, 74, 92, 105, 127
Everett, J., 50
Ewing, John, 70, 75
Fearon, Jackie, 148
Federation of East London Churches, 100

Federation of inner London churches, 116
Foreman, Margaret, 121
forward movement, 70
Fouracre, Roy, 108, 122, 123
Fox, Charles, 50, 107
Fox, R. W., 50
Fox, William chemist, 50, 107
Free Christian Union, 15
Freeman, Baptist weekly, 26
Fullerton, William, 48
Genesis London Ltd, 142
Giller, Gordon, 118–22
Girls' Brigade, 129
Girls' Life Brigade, 75, 76, 81, 83, 87, 90, 121, 127
Goddard & Phillips of Highgate, 113
Great Depression, 85
Great War, 73
grocery vouchers, 85
Hackney Road frontage, 33, 34, 39, 50, 67, 130–32, 142
Hale, Edwin (Ted), 105
Hall, Melanie, 139
Harnden, Joseph, 17
Harrison, Fred, 94, 96
Hasfield, Gloucs., 28, 31, 77
Hayden, Geoffrey, 113, 115
Hayes, Daniel, 67, 71, 74
healing, 38, 105, 115
Henstock, Paul and Lynda, 122–28
Hernandez, Freddy, 140, 141
Hewetson, James, 57
Hitchman, George, 109, 123
Hitchman, Joyce, 119
Hitchman, Len, 108
Hockridge-Omonuwa, Olivia, 141, 143, 145, 148
Holiday Homes scheme, 86
Holy Trinity, Hounslow, 110

House to House Visiting Agency, 65
Hudson, Sidney F., 103, 104, 108
Imperial Gas Company, 25
James, Ann, 136, 137
Janes, Mark, 145
Jellis, Terry, 111
Jones, Ena, 122
Jones, Gareth, 148, 151
Jones, Ken and Ena, 108
Jones, William C., 26
Journey in Prayer, 142
Julier, Violet, 87, 90, 115, 133, 137, 140, 143, 145
Kevan, Nathaniel, 9, 13, 17, 19–25
Kevan, Samuel, 21
Killen, Hugh, 19, 24
King, Geoffrey, 94, 100
Knibb, William, 8
Ladies Hall, 89
Lawrence, Fiona, 140, 141, 142, 143
Lea Bridge Demolition Company, 111
Leak, Dave and Louise, 148
Lecture Hall, 34, 70, 82, 83, 87, 95, 100, 103–5, 110, 120–22, 124, 126–35, 138, 139
Liberal Party, 107
Liberal Party, 49
Link, Frederick "Cuff", 73
Lloyd, Matthew architect, 139, 143
London Association of Strict Baptist Ministers and Churches, 19, 20
London Baptist Association, 60, 70, 72, 74, 75, 79, 84, 100, 101, 116, 117, 119, 138, 146, 147
London Music Festival, 105
London Music Hall, 82
London New Association of Strict and Particular Baptists, 20, 21
Lottery funding, 139
Maclaren, Alexander, 41
Magic Lantern, 34, 58
manses
  Chambord Street, 134, 137
  Forest Drive East, Leytonstone, 101, 104, 133
  Palestine Place, Cambridge Heath, 31
  Trafalgar Place East, 11
  Winston Road, Stoke Newington, 123
Manson, Peter, 122
Marchant, Colin, 137
Mariner, Joan, 108, 109
Marriage Act of 1835, 24
Martineau, James, 15
Mason's Court, 7, 24
McBain, Douglas, 132
membership, 9, 13, 15, 17, 20, 74, 81, 94, 101, 104, 120, 137, 147
Men's Club, 88
Mentone, France, 38
Miall, William, 13–24
Mildmay Hospital, 71, 82, 124, 129, 131, 132, 142
Mills, Kath, 135
Mills, Kathleen, 133, 141
Missions, 37, 51, 57, 73, 81
  Bethel Chapel, Austin Street, 57
  Brick Lane, 47, 51
  Collingwood Street, 57

Gibraltar Walk, 51, 106, 107
Hope Mission in Haggerston, 57
Hoxton House, 57, 76
Kingsland Road Hall, 36, 39, 51, 57, 58
Pownall Road, 72, 90, 105, 113
Queen's Road, 72, 90–92, 109
Shacklewell Street, 57
Shap Street, 57, 58, 76, 81, 84
Thorold Square, 16
Vincent Street, 57
Virginia Row, 57
Wellington Street, 57
Morris, Sydney G., 104
Mumby, Bill, 105
Naunton, Cotswolds, 28
Nicholls, Mike, 132
Old Nichol, 58, 87, 107, 151
Open Air Services, 36, 37, 47, 58, 76, 106, 108
open communion, 46
Orange, Dorothy 'Dolly', 104, 108
organ, 13, 52, 66, 87, 93, 110, 135
Parry, Sarah, 137–45
Particular Baptists, 19, 20, 21
Pask, Elizabeth, 24
Pask, Phebe, 24
Passmore, Joseph, 48
pastoral visiting, 11, 72, 82, 106, 117, 119, 132
Pat Took, 145
Peabody Buildings, Spitalfields, 33, 66
Pearson, Richard E., 81, 84, 87, 91, 106, 137

Perkins & Son, M. Trimming maker, 113
Perkins, Agnes (Aggie), 109
Perkins, William, 7, 113
Pettigrew, Emma, 140
pew rents, 26
Pilkington, Christina, 148
Pillow, Thomas, 13, 17, 22, 28, 29
politics, 24, 49, 60
Pollock, Lord Chief Justice, 27
Poor Fund, 36
Pope, William, 17
prayer, 9, 16, 20, 31, 32, 39, 46, 47, 64, 121, 126, 141, 142
Providence Chapel, 8, 10, 13, 15–33, 39, 67, 113
Providence Hall, Cumberland St., 8, 13, 16, 113
Rawdon Baptist College, 105, 109
Regent's Park College, 79, 132
Religious Tract Society, 65
Rest Centre, 94
Rhoden, Beryl, 121
Roberts, Hannah, 139
Robinson, Peter, 134–37
Rose, Miss Doris M., 82
Russell, John, 26, 28, 39, 42
Sale of Work, 87
Salmon, Agnes, 93
Sanalitro, Andrew, 139, 143, 145, 146, 148
Sayer, Len, 105, 138
School Hall 1890. *See* Lecture Hall
School Room 1844, 16, 17, 33, 39, 67
Scripture Examination, 58
seaside excursions, 50, 83, 84, 86

Shoreditch Council of Churches, 120
Shoreditch Town Hall, 32, 33, 37, 39, 42, 44, 67
Shoreditch Vestry, 25, 32
Shorey, John, 106, 111
Shosanya, David, 146, 150
Sick Benefits Society, 76
Simmonds, Bill, 94
Skerritt, Benjamin, 9
Smith, Charles, 17–23, 24
Smith, J. Manton, 48
Smith, James, 8, 11, 13, 14, 24
Sobey, Keith, 108, 118
Soul Survivor, 150
Spenser, Sam, artist, 150
Spirit Level, 141
Spurgeon, C. H., 22, 28, 29, 30, 34, 38, 48
Spurgeon's College, 28, 48, 68, 108, 109, 118, 122, 127, 132, 145
Spurgeon's College Society of Evangelists, 48
Spurgeon's Orphan Boys, 43
St Catherine's College, Oxford, 79
St Leonard's Church, Shoreditch, 7, 99, 129, 139
Street Pastors, 146
Strict Baptists, 19, 24, 29
Stride, Georgina, 145–48
Sunday School, 7, 15, 39, 51, 66, 76, 81, 84, 87, 94, 104, 105, 106, 108, 119, 122, 125, 126, 139, 141, 142, 148
Symons, W. J., 91, 95, 96, 101

Tab Centre, 8, 39, 53, 77, 138–51
Tab Create, 149
Tab People, 136, 137, 139, 140, 141, 149
Took, Pat, 137
Tract Society, 37
Tredinnik, Susan, 74
Tuff, Rachel, 31
Tunde, Sam, 135, 137, 143
Tyler, A. H., 75, 84, 91
War Damage money, 100, 104, 107, 110, 113
Warnock, Clare, 139, 143
West Ham Central Mission, 79
Weston, David, 108, 122, 120–27, 134
Weston, Harry, 102–6
Weston, Joyce, 108, 129
Weston, Lillian, 104, 108, 109
William Hill organ builders, 66
women deacons, 65, 100, 104
Women's Meeting, 76, 81, 82, 86, 92, 109
Woodbridge, Kathleen (Mills), 109
Woodman, Charles Bathurst, 7
Woolvett, Fred G., 113
Woolvett, Matthew, 114
Worship Academy, 147, 148
Wren, Job, 33, 50, 57, 66, 67, 77, 80
Young Men's Institute, 74
young people, 36, 42, 72, 76, 83, 94, 105, 120, 138, 147
Young, Dr William, 94, 96, 97
youth work, 119